THE JOURNAL OF THE ASSOCIATION OF MOVING IMAGE ARCHIVISTS

VINGIMAGETHE MOVINGIMAGE THE MOVINGIMAGETHE MOV

FALL 2022

The Moving Image (ISSN 1532-3978) is published twice a year in spring and fall by the University of Minnesota Press, 111 Third Avenue South, Suite 290, Minneapolis, MN 55401-2520. http://www.upress.umn.edu

Published in cooperation with the Association of Moving Image Archivists (AMIA). Members of AMIA receive the journal as one of the benefits of membership. For further information about membership, contact the Association of Moving Image Archivists, 1313 North Vine Street, Hollywood, CA 90028 (or email amia@amianet.org or visit http://www.amianet.org).

Postmaster: Send address changes to *The Moving Image,* University of Minnesota Press, 111 Third Avenue South, Suite 290, Minneapolis, MN 55401-2520.

Inquiries and information about manuscript submissions should be sent to editor@themovingimage.org. All manuscripts should be submitted as a Microsoft Word email attachment, double-spaced throughout, using 12-point type with 1-inch margins, using the *Chicago Manual of Style,* 17th edition.

Review copies of DVDs or books should be sent to the AMIA office at 1313 North Vine Street, Hollywood, CA 90028, USA.

Please allow a minimum of 4 months for editorial consideration.

Address subscription orders, changes of address, and business correspondence (including requests for permission and advertising orders) to *The Moving Image,* University of Minnesota Press, 111 Third Avenue South, Suite 290, Minneapolis, MN 55401-2520.

Subscriptions: For our current subscription rates please see our website: http://www.upress.umn.edu. *The Moving Image* is a benefit of membership in the Association of Moving Image Archivists.

Digital subscriptions to *The Moving Image* are available online through the Project MUSE Journals Collection Program at https://muse.jhu.edu/.

Most images reproduced in *The Moving Image* are available to view in color in the electronic edition of *The Moving Image,* accessible via Project MUSE.

Founded in 1991, the **Association of Moving Image Archivists** is the world's largest professional association devoted to film, television, video, and digital image preservation. Dedicated to issues surrounding the safekeeping of visual history, this journal covers topics such as the role of moving image archives and collection in the writing of history, technical and practical articles on research and development in the field, in-depth examinations of specific preservation and restoration projects, and behind-the-scenes looks at the techniques used to preserve and restore our moving image heritage.

Heather Heckman *University of South Carolina*

Jan-Christopher Horak *JCH Archival Consulting*

Eric Hoyt *University of Wisconsin–Madison*

Luna Hupperetz *University of Amsterdam/Vrije Universiteit*

Jennifer Jenkins *University of Arizona*

Jimi Jones *University of Illinois*

Peter Kaufman *Intelligent TV*

Andrea Leigh *Library of Congress*

Bert Lyons *AVP*

Mike Mashon *Library of Congress*

Jan Müller *Regional Public Broadcasting Foundation (RPO)*

Charles Musser *Yale University*

Joshua Ng *Archives New Zealand Te Rua Mahara o te Kāwanatanga*

Kassandra O'Connell *Irish Film Institute*

Miriam Posner *University of California, Los Angeles*

Rick Prelinger *University of California, Santa Cruz*

Meredith Reese *LA Phil*

Lauren Sorensen *Whirl-i-Gig*

Katherine Spring *Wilfrid Laurier University*

Shelley Stamp *University of California, Santa Cruz*

Rachael Stoeltje *Indiana University*

Dan Streible *New York University*

Kara Van Malssen *AVP*

Haidee Wasson *Concordia University*

Mark Williams *Dartmouth University*

Tami Williams *University of Wisconsin–Milwaukee*

Joshua Yumibe *Michigan State University*

Patricia Zimmermann *Ithaca College*

EDITOR'S FOREWORD

Devin Orgeron   vii

FEATURES

Locating Early Amateur Fiction Films: Using Archival Sources to Uncover the S. W. Childs Jr. Collection

Brian Meacham and Ryan Shand   1

Exile, Archives, and Transnational Film History: The Returns of Chilean Exile Cinema

José Miguel Palacios   29

Piracy and Media Archival Access in the Digital Era

Micah Gottlieb   59

COLLECTIONS

Documented Aliens: Encyclopaedia Britannica's Revolutionary Foreign-Language Instruction Films of the Post-Sputnik Era

Geoff Alexander   78

Report on Current Film Cleaning Practices and Issues: AMIA Preservation Committee Film Cleaning Workgroup, June 2022

Susan P. Etheridge, Anne Gant, Diana Little, and Julia Mettenleiter   91

REVIEWS

BOOK

Experiencing Cinema: Participatory Film Cultures, Immersive Media and the Experience Economy, by Emma Pett
Bloomsbury Academic, 2021
Hannah Lee   102

The Rise and Fall of Max Linder: The First Cinema Celebrity, by Lisa Stein Haven
BearManor Media, 2021
Ulrich Ruedel   105

The Greatest Films Never Seen: The Film Archive and the Copyright Smokescreen, by Claudy Op den Kamp
Amsterdam University Press, 2018
Matthias Smith   107

DVD/BLU-RAY

Zander the Great
Beverly of Graustark
DVD/Blu-ray distributed by Undercrank Productions, 2022
Aurore Spiers   110

REVIEW ESSAY

Barbara Hammer and Maya Deren
Bart Testa   114

Editor's Foreword

DEVIN ORGERON

We at *The Moving Image* are acutely aware of your reading needs. And, while we've neglected them for months, we are back in full force! We know you just finished reading issue 22.1. Are you even ready for issue 22.2? Regardless, here it is!

Our kidding in issue 22.1 about "normal" issues, of course, extends to the issue you hold in your hands. And, all kidding aside, I think this is what we love about *TMI*.

This issue begins with a cowritten feature by **Brian Meacham** and **Ryan Shand** that charts early amateur filmmaking practices on university campuses in the United States and the United Kingdom. Collaborative, transnational, and both within and about the archives, Meacham and Shand's contribution here is both an ideal *TMI* form and a wonderfully narrated account of a collection coming into view before our (collective) eyes.

José Miguel Palacios brings us "Exile, Archives, and Transnational Film History: The Returns of Chilean Exile Cinema." Beautifully written and expertly researched, this piece examines the current condition of Chilean exile cinema across multiple archives throughout the world, focusing on what Palacios refers to as the recent "phenomenon of return" to several major archives and museums: archival returns. Palacios elegantly allows readers to reconsider their ideas about exile and to think about the impact these notions have on the archive.

Our Features section concludes with a provocative piece by new author **Micah Gottlieb.** "Piracy and Media Archival Access in the Digital Era" is part research article, part investigation/instigation. A fresh look at the concept (practical and theoretical) of piracy, Gottlieb's piece focuses on the phenomenon's relationship to archives, especially since Covid-19. It's a piece that will get us thinking, and talking. I suspect it will also make us look forward to Gottlieb's future contributions.

Our Collections section boasts a wonderful and unique exploration of a genre of film some of us have not thought about in many, many years: language instruction films. **Geoff Alexander,** true to form, offers a detailed and sometimes surprising history of Encyclopaedia Britannica Films' ambitious 191-film effort and makes a plea for their continued importance—offering them up, so to speak, for future generations of scholarly investigation. A longtime friend of AMIA, Alexander, in "Documented Aliens: Encyclopaedia Britannica's Revolutionary Foreign-Language Instruction Films of the Post-Sputnik Era," does what he does best: he nudges us into paying attention in and outside of class.

We've also included in our Collections section the coauthored "Report on Current Film Cleaning Practices and Issues: AMIA Preservation Committee Film Cleaning Workgroup, June 2022." Here **Susan P. Etheridge, Anne Gant, Diana Little,** and **Julia Mettenleiter** provide the results from and offer perspective on a 2021 survey conducted by the AMIA Preservation Committee Film Cleaning Workgroup. We include it in our Collections section because we suspect it will be almost universally relevant to our readership, many of whom find themselves functioning within, as the authors phrase it, "a matrix of suboptimal solutions." It's the real world—and work like this reminds us of its limitations.

I want to wrap up this introduction with a word of thanks. I joked a bit in the previous issue about the delays that find us releasing two issues back to back. Of note, to my mind at least, is the fact that our delays at no point had anything to do with a lack of enthusiasm for TMI's mission or a lack of material. On the contrary, we had amassed so much material that we needed to split it across two issues, and we have three future issues well under way. I'm grateful for this faith in our efforts, and I'm humbled by our contributors' and readers' patience as we collectively worked to navigate a not-quite-post-Covid-19 landscape. The way we do business of any sort, as our Conversations section in issue 22.1 so nicely illustrates, has been altered. I'm also grateful to a team of folks at AMIA (particularly Laura Rooney) and specifically the core *TMI* team (Liza Palmer and Brian Real) for providing much-needed support and assistance as I regained my own ever-tenuous footing. It's been an exceptionally long couple of years, folks. But I'm glad we have a record of this critical work in our field going on in spite of it. So thank you AMIA, *TMI,* and our readers!

And please remember: there's *always* an open call at *The Moving Image*!

Devin Orgeron is editor of *The Moving Image*, Professor Emeritus of Film and Media Studies at North Carolina State University, and chair of the Northeast Historic Film Summer Symposium, which takes place in late July in Bucksport, Maine. He is the author of *Road Movies* (2008) and editor of *Learning with the Lights Off* (2012).

LOCATING EARLY AMATEUR FICTION FILMS

BRIAN MEACHAM
AND RYAN SHAND

Using Archival Sources to
Uncover the S. W. Childs Jr.
Collection

Film archivists and historians have been active in researching amateur cinema for approximately forty years. One of the challenges in researching this sector is that numerous case studies could potentially be investigated. Archives increasingly hold a wide range of different types of amateur films, including home movies, community films, and competition entries. Given this diverse range of amateur material, how can we decide which case studies to prioritize? Answering this question can be difficult. Each archivist or historian will have their own reasons, sometimes pragmatic and sometimes theoretical, for focusing on particular topics. However, we have identified an area of research that might be particularly useful in understanding the early history of amateur cinema. In this article, we outline the history of amateur filmmaking on university campuses. We seek to establish two main points: first, the importance of campus-based cine-clubs to the early development of the amateur cine movement and, second, the role that both archivists and historians can have in locating these amateur films.

In the two sections that follow, we reflect on what we have discovered on these topics over the eight years and detail the research methods we used to locate this information. The first section is written by Ryan Shand, a film historian based in the United Kingdom who is particularly interested in exploring the early history of amateur filmmaking on university campuses in both the United Kingdom and the United States. Shand explains how he first became aware of the potential benefits of investigating this topic, before demonstrating how studies of wider significance can emerge from a highly focused case study. In our second section, Brian Meacham, a film archivist based in the United States, details how access to digitized archival sources enabled him to gather relevant information about these amateur productions from the 1920s, which subsequently informed a targeted acquisition strategy. This article charts a project that began as an academic study but, over time, became a research collaboration, resulting in the acquisition, preservation, and exhibition of a collection of pioneering American amateur films that might have otherwise been considered lost. As this is a cowritten article, in this introduction and the conclusion, we refer to ourselves in the first person plural; however, within the two sections that follow, we switch to the first-person singular to detail our respective research methods.

THE FILM HISTORIAN'S ACCOUNT

New research avenues can often emerge from unexplored aspects of previous projects. In April 2014, I visited the Northeast Historic Film archive in Maine to spend a week re-searching amateur films and videos made by children and teenagers. I made this trip to Bucksport with my colleague from a four-year research project that was approaching its final stages.[1] On our first day of research, David Weiss, the executive director of Northeast Historic Film, mentioned that the collection held an amateur film from England. However, his caveat was that it was made by university rather than high school students. Although it was not strictly within the remit we were exploring in our current research project, I was intrigued enough to set aside time to watch the film before I left.

The student film was called *Counterpoint* (Roy Lockwood, 1929). When viewing it for the first time, I discovered that it was a romantic drama featuring some sophisticated visual experimentation and employing a flashback structure to tell its story. The film was also intriguing in a number of respects, raising questions both during the viewing itself and on later reflection. First, it was made in Oxford, England, but is now housed in a film

Figure 1. Still from *Counterpoint* (Roy Lockwood, 1929). Courtesy of Northeast Historic Film, Roy Lockwood Collection.

archive in the United States. How did this amateur film find its way to Maine? Second, it was a fiction film made during the 1920s. In my previous research into amateur cinema in the United Kingdom, the earliest amateur fiction films were mostly from the 1930s. Third, the running time of the VHS version I watched was approximately forty-two minutes, but the story did not reach a conclusion, and there were no closing credits. Did other reels exist, or was this film incomplete? Although these were certainly interesting research questions, I put them to the back of my mind and returned to focusing on films made by students in American high schools.

Once I returned to the United Kingdom, I consulted a few print and online resources to see if I could find any references to *Counterpoint*. I searched the online catalogs of regional and national archives; however, prints of *Counterpoint* did not seem to exist in the United Kingdom, and scholars of amateur cinema had not made reference to it so far. When I did find relevant references to the early development of amateur cinema in the United Kingdom, they were in books published soon after the events being described actually happened. For example, in 1932, Marjorie Agnes Lovell

Burgess wrote *A Popular Account of the Development of the Amateur Ciné Movement in Great Britain*. In this book, she states,

> I believe the first amateur cine club in the world was started in Cambridge in 1923, under the title of the Cambridge Kiné Club. Amateur film making activities first began in this country about 1922. Filming began at Oxford in 1924.[2]

The tentative language of this quotation is significant. Burgess was personally involved in these fledgling activities, and her account has a distinctly subjective quality. Our knowledge of the early history of the amateur cine movement in the United Kingdom has remained relatively provisional even until recently. For example, in her book *Amateur Film: Meaning and Practice, 1927–77,* Heather Norris Nicholson writes,

> The BFI's *Catalogue of the National Film Library* (1936) lists *The Witch's Fiddle* (Dir. P. Le Neve Foster, 1924) as the first film produced by Cambridge University Film Society (aka Kinema Club). *Amateur Films* 1:7 (1929) also mentions *Big Dog* (Dir. Rudolph Messel) and comments: "one of the original Oxford amateur cinematographers in 1924." No further information about early activity at Oxford has surfaced in my research.[3]

At conferences and workshops, Norris Nicholson and I discussed the fact that we knew the titles of these early films but not where any prints were held. At that point, I did not know that a print of *The Witch's Fiddle* was indeed held by the British Film Institute National Archive. This title is thought to be the first student film ever made (at least in the United Kingdom), and it is now available to view on the British Film Institute YouTube channel.[4] It is clearly significant that we can now watch one of the pioneering amateur films at the click of a button, though for many years it was assumed to be just another lost film, even by scholars who specialized in this topic.

Following this initial research at Northeast Historic Film, I became increasingly convinced that *Counterpoint* offered a potentially significant window into amateur film culture during the 1920s. The fact that this was an amateur fiction film was even more intriguing, because it had become evident that despite often being part of archival collections, many archivists are still unsure of amateur films' wider cultural value. Guy Edmonds summed this situation up succinctly when writing, "Close inspection of archive holdings reveals, however, that they *are* often there, though not *because* they are amateur fiction films, and certainly not valued on that basis."[5] Along these lines, part of my interest was to understand how this amateur fiction film had become part of the collection at Northeast Historic Film. Therefore, the next year, I decided to apply for the William O'Farrell Fellowship, organized by Northeast Historic Film, to do more research on the film. This annual fellowship "is awarded to an individual engaged in research toward a publication, production, or presentation based on moving image history and culture, particularly amateur and nontheatrical film."[6] Even at this early stage, I sensed that the film was probably indicative of wider trends within that decade. In my application, I wrote,

> I would like to make *Counterpoint* better known. To do this, my research methodology would be to combine close analysis with a contextual study. Initially, research time would be devoted to the aesthetics of the film; specifically shot selections, narrative development and genre concerns. At the same time, this close analysis needs to be coupled with a concern to establish how this film fits into the wider context of amateur filmmaking at elite educational institutions in the 1920s and early 1930s; comparisons will be made with filmmaking at nearby Cambridge University, but also the Ivy League cine clubs in the United States.

This approach, which aimed to combine the analysis of individual films with attention to sociocultural factors, was partly a methodological preference—I tend to study aesthetics within historical frameworks. However, it also indicated a potential way to orient my research from more practical perspectives. I hoped to use the case study of *Counterpoint* to find out more about the film but also to learn new techniques for researching early amateur films from the 1920s.

I was successful in my application and was able to start planning a follow-up visit to Northeast Historic Film. I also received the additional assistance of a travel grant from university research funds, which helped to cover the cost of the transatlantic flights.[7] I arrived back in Bucksport in August 2015 to spend two weeks pursuing this new research avenue. On returning to the archive, I quickly learned that I had only seen approximately half of the film on my previous viewing. Since my last visit, the archival staff had made me a DVD copy of the complete film, which I was able to watch repeatedly at my leisure over the next two weeks. I also discovered much more about the material history of the film.

On my previous trip to the archive, I had wondered why this film from England was now in an archive in Maine. On this return trip, I learned that later in his life, Roy Lockwood was a recreational sailor, so he retired to the coastal town of Yarmouth, which is approximately ninety miles south of Bucksport. The film was donated to the archive by Roy Lockwood himself in May 1993. Lockwood asked for two VHS copies and said that the archive could keep the film print. There are no other films from the Lockwood Collection at Northeast Historic Film. When Joe Gardner, the technical services manager, talked me through his inspection of the *Counterpoint* film print, he confirmed that the splicing indicated that it was the original reversal. The damage to parts of the reversal suggested that it was either shown repeatedly or was perhaps shown on an older projector. Overall, the complete film was approximately two thousand feet in length, which would make the running time approximately eighty-eight minutes when projected. Therefore *Counterpoint* was more than double the length of the extract I had watched the previous year. Most intriguingly for the exhibition history of the film, Joe also noticed that the Kodak date code on the film stock revealed that an early sequence was in fact shot in 1930. Therefore certain sequences were shot and added after the principal photography.

This information corresponds with one of the few references to *Counterpoint* that I was able to locate. I discovered that Roy Lockwood and his film were mentioned in a manual called *Filmcraft: The Art of Picture Production,* which was written by the professional film director Adrian Brunel.[8] Brunel introduces the chapter written by Lockwood, called "That Assistant Director," in the following way:

> Mr. Lockwood began to acquire his knowledge of films at Oxford, where he made "Counterpoint," a six-reeler (16 mm.) film, which was shown in London in 1930. Later he went to the British International Studios at Elstree and eventually worked as assistant director on several productions. For over a year he has been editing films for me—and I hope he will continue to do so.[9]

This short paragraph confirmed both the estimated length of *Counterpoint* and that it was publicly screened in London in 1930. Unfortunately, the chapter that Lockwood wrote on his subsequent experience of being a professional assistant director does not provide any further information on his time as an amateur filmmaker at Oxford. In addition, I was able to find references to Roy Lockwood in Adrian Brunel's other books, *Nice Work* and *Film Production*—works that are available in the Northeast Historic Film library.[10] Although these references were informative, I could not locate any further information about the London screening of *Counterpoint*. The distribution history of *Counterpoint* might be traceable by consulting early amateur film magazines published in the United Kingdom, but while one research avenue closed for the time being, another possible line of inquiry began to open up. I set myself the task of finding out whether American students were also attempting feature-length amateur film productions during the 1920s.

Campus-Based Cine-Clubs in the United States

Although my initial research on amateur filmmaking in the 1920s focused on the book collection in the Northeast Historic Film library, I was increasingly drawn to exploring the library's extensive collection of early film journals. These included film magazines like *Amateur Cine World, The Amateur Photographer and Cinematographer, Home Movies, Home Movies and Home Talkies,* and *Movie Makers.* Both *Amateur Cine World* and *Home Movies and Home Talkies* were British magazines, so the fact that they were part of archival collections in the United States attests to the transatlantic nature of amateur film culture. Indeed, these magazines regularly covered amateur activity in each other's countries, so that their readers could stay informed of recent developments. I even found mention of the early activities of the Cambridge University Kinema Club in *Movie Makers,* a journal that was published in the United States. In a short report on British cine-club news, it was noted that "this university, so far as we know, was the first to produce an amateur photoplay."[11]

After a few days of researching these paper archives, I found that it was a time-consuming process to look through numerous volumes of magazines without having specific information to help me locate the articles of particular relevance. I would be able to focus on this task for only two weeks, before returning to other work-related activities back in the United Kingdom, so I had to use this research time as productively as possible. Therefore my planned research methodology was aided greatly when Karan Sheldon, cofounder of Northeast Historic Film, asked if I knew about the Media History Digital Library.[12] I had not explored this website before, so it was immediately clear that it would enable me to search for relevant information on early amateur filmmaking in a much more comprehensive way than was previously possible. For example, its "Non-Theatrical Film Collection" allows users to search digitized issues of important magazines, such as *Movie Makers* and *The Amateur Photographer and Cinematographer.* This online digitization initiative means that these American amateur film magazines are currently much more accessible than British equivalents, such as *Amateur Cine World,* a situation that could be addressed in the future.

One way of utilizing the vast resources of the Media History Digital Library is to experiment with a variety of keyword searches to locate specific information. In my notebook, I wrote a list of the so-called Ivy League universities, including Brown, Columbia, Cornell, Dartmouth, Harvard, the University of Pennsylvania, Princeton, and Yale. Then I began doing searches using the names of these universities, along with other keywords, such as "student films" and "amateur filmmaking." When I started to look through the recommended articles in these journals, I could see that the information in Heather Norris Nicholson's quotation was largely confirmed. In this respect, Frederick James Smith's short article from *Photoplay* magazine was a gold mine of information:

> Now that PHOTOPLAY'S second contest has moved into history, it is interesting to look over the records of amateur activities. The amateur film for instance, has reached a high point of development in colleges and universities.
>
> The first collegiate production on record with the Amateur Cinema League is "The Witches' Fiddle," produced by the Kinema Club of Cambridge University, England, in 1922. This was made on standard width film, as was the club's second production, "A Miss in May Week." A club at Oxford University was formed shortly after and then Harvard Workshop entered the field in America with a 35 millimeter production.
>
> That was the beginning. Amateur film work began to be taken up by universities all over the world. The Purity Players of Yale produced Fielding's "Tom Jones" in an interesting way and the film attracted wide attention.
>
> The students of Colgate made "Roommates," an amateur group of the University of Southern California produced "The Sporting Chance." Groups have been active at the University of Minnesota, Stanford, Princeton, the University of Virginia, Amherst, Dartmouth and the University of Oregon.[13]

This article provides an invaluable comparative analysis of the respective amateur filmmaking activities being initiated almost simultaneously in the United Kingdom and the United States. The author notes that the information on the British cine-clubs was verified by the American organization for amateur filmmaking, highlighting that the "first collegiate production on record with the Amateur Cinema League" was indeed *The Witch's Fiddle,* which suggests that this information was viewed as significant to tracing the early development of the organized amateur cine sector on both sides of the Atlantic.[14]

This quotation proved to be a catalyst for much of the research I was able to complete while based in Bucksport. It lists precise dates on the formation of these clubs and the titles of their early productions, suggesting that *The Witch's Fiddle* might have been made either one or two years before Marjorie Agnes Lovell Burgess and Heather Norris Nicholson cited in their provisional historical accounts. The alternative spelling of *The Witch's Fiddle,* which is here titled *The Witches' Fiddle,* could be a copyediting error. In relation to my further investigation of the early amateur films made by students in the

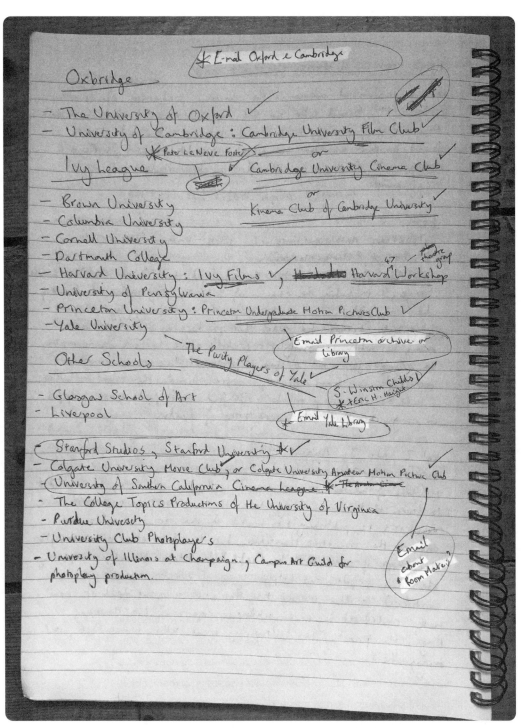

Figure 2. A page from Ryan Shand's notebook while he was researching early amateur film clubs based at universities.

United States, this article specifically named the Purity Players of Yale's production of *Tom Jones* and Colgate University's *Roommates* as pioneering titles.

Notably, this article asserts that the first two Cambridge University Kinema Club titles were photographed using standard-width film, which demonstrates that amateur film activity was not dependent on the introduction of small-gauge technology. However, reversal-processed 16mm safety film was introduced by Kodak a year later in 1923.[15] The article also alludes to other universities, outside of the Oxbridge and Ivy League institutions, that similarly had students who were involved in early amateur activities. I attempted keyword searches for some of these colleges and universities in the Media History Digital Library database, as well as others mentioned in similar articles, including Illinois at Urbana-Champaign and Purdue. During my remaining time at Northeast Historic Film, I was able to use this research process to compile an initial chronology of the fifteen early amateur films made by American students in the 1920s and early 1930s, which I intended to locate, if it was possible.

Once I returned to the United Kingdom, I was able to build on the research I had completed in Bucksport. At this stage, I focused on gathering the contact details of university libraries or nearby archives that could possibly have in their collections any of the amateur films identified. I planned to contact institutions based in both the United Kingdom and the United States. Upon review of this chronological list, it was evident that five amateur moviemaking clubs based in the United States were of particular interest. To demonstrate how I approached this stage of my research, I detail this process with reference to Colgate University and Yale University.

The *Photoplay* article highlighted two American titles, namely, *Roommates* and *Tom Jones*. Focusing on the Colgate University Amateur Motion Picture Club for a moment, in my subsequent research at Northeast Historic Film, I learned that, in addition to *Roommates,* the club produced another film, called *A Day in College* (1928). Following an initial inquiry submitted through the Colgate University Libraries website, I was contacted by the head of special collections and university archivist. I had emailed explaining who I was, what I was working on, and what films I was searching for. I concluded the email by writing, "I was wondering if you had heard of the Colgate University Amateur Motion Picture Club before? Does your library have a film collection and if so does it have these particular films, or any other early student films from the 1920s or 1930s? If not, it would be great if you could please put me in contact with a local film archive that might be able to help." The head of special collections replied to tell me that the department had completed an inventory of its motion picture film holdings the previous year, but unfortunately, those two titles did not appear to be there. In fact, they had never heard of the Amateur Motion Picture Club before but would be on the lookout for materials about it. While it was disappointing that the films of this amateur moviemaking club were not available, it was somewhat gratifying to think that they might now be on the radar of the Colgate University Libraries archivists going forward. Around the same time as this email exchange with Colgate University staff, I initiated a similar dialogue with librarians at Yale University.

While based in Bucksport the previous summer, I had been able to gather more information about the Purity Players of Yale University. S. Winston Childs Jr. of Norfolk, Connecticut, founded this club in March 1925, and over the next couple years, it produced five amateur fiction films: *Tracks of Blood* (1925), *Passion's Toll* (circa 1926), *Steppes of Silence* (circa 1926), *The Horsemen of Death* (circa 1926), and *Tom Jones* (1927). Like *Counterpoint,* which was made around the same time in the United Kingdom, both *The Horsemen of Death* and *Tom Jones* were photographed using 16mm stock and, even more significantly, had feature-length running times. Whereas the club's first three productions were short films, *The Horsemen of Death* was approximately two thousand feet long, but *Tom Jones* had a running time more than double that, at approximately five thousand feet. At last, I had found confirmation that there were indeed American equivalents of *Counterpoint,* but I did not know if copies of these amateur feature films still existed.

I remained hopeful that the Purity Players films would be available to view due to articles that detailed prints of *Tom Jones* being offered to two archival collections. The pages of *Amateur Movie Maker* reported that "Childs owns the negative of the reels, although a print has been offered to the Yale Library to be placed in the Archives."[16] A few year later, *Movie Makers* magazine confirmed that Childs donated prints of *Tom Jones* and *The Horsemen of Death* to the Amateur Cinema League's Club Film Library.[17] This information encouraged me to email Yale University in April 2016 to ask if it had further information on the Purity Players.

I received a reply from the chief research archivist in the Manuscripts and Archives department, who confirmed that Starling Winston Childs Jr. graduated from Yale in 1927 but that there was no information about the Purity Players in his class book or in the annual *Yale Banner.* However, more promisingly, there were many entries on the Purity Players in the Yale Daily News Historical Archive, which is available to search via the Yale University Library Digital Collections website.[18] This student newspaper had contemporary articles on the Purity Players, in particular, their premiere screening of *Tom Jones* on the Yale campus in June 1927.

In addition, I asked Yale University staff if they knew of any nearby archives that might have collected amateur films from this decade. This was the turning point of my research so far, as they suggested that I should contact Brian Meacham, the archive and special collections manager at the Yale Film Study Center (now the Yale Film Archive). Helpfully, Brian's contact details were listed on the center website, so I emailed him to find out what he might know about the Purity Players.

THE FILM ARCHIVIST'S ACCOUNT

"Deep in a Closet There Are Films": Recovering the Work of an Amateur Film Pioneer

"I was wondering if you had heard of the Purity Players of Yale before?" I had been at my new job as archive and special collections manager of the Yale Film Archive for less than two years, and I had to confess to the author of this inquiry, Ryan Shand, that indeed I had not heard of this group of amateur filmmakers and could find no films credited to them in our collection. Shand, at the time a researcher at the University of the West of Scotland, had come across their name while researching the early history of student filmmaking in the United States and the United Kingdom as a fellow at Northeast Historic Film the previous year and was investigating whether any of the troupe's work still existed.

The group's founder, S. Winston Childs Jr., was a member of the Yale class of 1927, and, spurred by Shand's inquiry, I set about trying to track down his family and possibly his films. By the following month, I had made contact via email with his nephew and had discovered that S. W. Childs Jr., who went by "Wink" or "Winkie," was a part of a multigenerational Yale family. Childs's grandfather, Albert H. Childs, was a member of the class of 1861, and his father, son, and grandson all attended the university as well. Childs's mother, Jane Coffin Childs, died of cancer in 1936, and her husband, S. W. Childs Sr., along with his sister-in-law Alice Coffin, started the Jane Coffin Childs Memorial Fund for Medical Research, a Yale-based foundation, still active today, which has supported hundreds of research fellowships over the last eighty-five years. Despite these deep connections, though, none of the work of S. Winston Childs Jr. and his fellow Purity Players was held in the collections of the Yale University Library, and Childs was, as far as I could tell, nearly unknown in the long history of filmmaking at Yale. As I would discover over the following years, Childs and his family and friends were enthusiastic, prolific, and skilled amateur filmmakers, the creative force behind one of the earliest student feature films made in the United States, and forgotten pioneers who were recognized in their time for ambitious and witty works of early small-gauge filmmaking.

Although an initial search through the database of the film archive (then known as the Yale Film Study Center) and the catalogs of various repositories in the Yale

University Library system turned up no results for Childs's films, a similar search in the literature of Childs's era brought a much different result: S. W. Childs Jr. and the Purity Players were a fairly regular presence in the pages of *Amateur Movie Maker* (later *Movie Makers*) in the 1920s and 1930s, also making appearances in *American Cinematographer* and other publications.

My email inquiries to members of the Childs family eventually put me in touch with Childs's daughter-in-law Hope Childs, who emailed me a brief but tantalizing response: "Deep in a closet there are films." She was interested in donating the films to the archive and, by fall 2016, we had set a time for me to visit her at home, S. W. Childs's former house, in Norfolk, Connecticut, to pick up the films she had gathered together. When I arrived on a snowy morning in November, I was greeted by a dining room table covered with films in boxes, in cans, and on reels (Figure 3). Her father-in-law's "film room," as it was known, had been converted into a bathroom in the 1980s, relegating his films to a closet, which Hope had emptied for my visit. I took everything that had been found, leaving with thirteen boxes of 16mm film, a treasure trove of more than 450 reels shot between the 1920s and 1960s. (The haul also included one small box of decomposing 35mm nitrate film, including just one salvageable reel, on stock manufactured in 1924. This tinted reel of an unidentified couple on horseback was donated to the Library of Congress.) Five years later, having inventoried the last of the reels, I am now able to chart the history of Childs's work in film, from his youth in Connecticut through his years leading a student filmmaking group in college and as a prolific amateur filmmaker with his wife, Cynthia, in the 1930s and 1940s.

The Purity Players

Shand's initial inquiry named five Purity Players productions: *Tracks of Blood, Passion's Toll, Steppes of Silence, The Horsemen of Death,* and *Tom Jones,* the last being described as a feature-length adaptation of Henry Fielding's 1749 novel. Among the reels in Hope Childs's donation, seemingly complete copies of three of these titles were found, with *Tracks of Blood* and *The Horsemen of Death* missing. In addition to these Purity Players productions, the collection contained the work of Childs's later production company, the Cynniewink Ciners. A portmanteau of the nicknames "Cynnie" and "Wink," the group's name is first found, appropriately, on the film documenting Wink and Cynthia's 1929 wedding, *The "Cynniewink" Sets Sail* (1929). The Childses' postgraduation filmmaking collective involved friends and family and produced a number of short films, including the award-winning 1932 film *I'd Be Delighted To!* and a follow-up, *Seductio ad Absurdum* (1940).

Figure 3. A dining room table covered with films in boxes, in cans, and on reels. Photograph by Brian Meacham.

In addition to the collected works of the Purity Players and the Cynniewink Ciners, the Childs Collection contains hundreds of rolls of home movies shot between the
1920s and 1960s, from Norfolk and New Haven, Connecticut, to international locations
including Canada, England, Japan, Cuba, and India. Childs, who went on to manage
Home Film Libraries and sit on its board of directors as it became rebranded as Films
Inc., meticulously documented his travels on film and also enjoyed trying out various
different film technologies and formats as they were released. The Childs home movie
collection includes not only color reversal and black-and-white reversal stocks but also
films shot on Kodacolor, Vitacolor, Agfa Plenachrome, and Kodak Reversal Sound Re-
cording film, among others.

Born in Lynn, Massachusetts, on July 4, 1904, Charles Starling Winston Childs
Jr. grew up in Norfolk, Connecticut, and was a cinema enthusiast and amateur filmmaker
from an early age. In 1925, he and his friends in Norfolk founded the Purity Players, a
group of amateur cinema enthusiasts who wrote, produced, directed, and acted in their
own 16mm productions. In an *Amateur Movie Makers* article that noted the premiere
screening of its 1927 film *Tom Jones,* Childs provided an account of the group's formation
and a description of its previous work:

> In March, 1925, a few friends and myself were up at Norfolk, Conn., and, having
> nothing better to do, we decided to film a movie. In a moment of inspiration we
> called it "Tracks of Blood" and attempted to burlesque the hard-ridin' two-fisted
> western thrillers. From this humble origin was born the organization known as
> the Purity Players. We consider ourselves somewhat in the light of pioneers in
> the field of amateur motion picture production.[19]

Unfortunately, *Tracks of Blood* was not found in the collection, but the group's next film
was another western adventure, this time about a mining inheritance, called *Passion's
Toll.* As Childs writes, looking back at *Tracks of Blood,*

> we saw many "rough" spots in the photoplay, action, and plot, which we felt
> could be eradicated to some extent in another trial, [so] we forthwith began
> to plan for "Passion's Toll." For the first time, girls were admitted to the Purity
> Players. Although the underlying theme of the picture was still one of burlesque,
> its importance lies in the fact that the story was longer, the plot more intricate,
> and the photography much better.[20]

The Purity Players' second film is an ambitious twenty-five-minute production that includes a lengthy chase that begins on foot, then transitions to horses, cars, and, finally, a biplane. Childs's Yale friend Ben Spock, later better known as the internationally renowned pediatrician and author Dr. Benjamin Spock, is credited as art director on the film and plays the role of the villain Ben Rice.[21] *Passion's Toll* tells the story of young Alma Mater, who travels west to Haystack, Colorado, to look after her father's failing mine. She meets Ed Hawkes, who helps her escape from Rice's plot to blow up the mine and kill her, to disguise the fact that the mine has failed. Childs himself plays one of the unnamed masked men who help rescue Hawkes from Rice's clutches.

The next year, inspired by winter weather, the Purity Players embarked on its next production, *Steppes of Silence.* The film tells the story of the feuding Yagustynka and Chenstohova families and the young man and woman who dare to defy their families and fall in love. As Childs described it in *Amateur Movie Maker,*

> in the winter of 1926, as there had been heavy snowfalls, our minds jumped at the possibility of burlesquing a Russian tragedy to be called "Steppes of Silence." Realizing that there would be but one day in which to film this picture, we spent many weeks previously in constructing the plot, outlining each scene in detail and writing the subtitles.[22]

The film featured the Purity Players' first attempts at filming an indoor scene, which, due to the group's limited technical abilities, Childs deemed "somewhat unintelligible."[23] More successful was another leap forward for the troupe: its first use of double exposure, in the climactic death scene of the hero and heroine, used to give the impression that Hanka had joined her lover Ploshka on the pyre on which he'd been burned alive.

A complete print of the Purity Players' next film, *The Horsemen of Death,* is also missing from the collection, but the donation did include a few tantalizing clues. First, in an unlabeled can found in a box of miscellaneous scraps of film were fifteen seconds of the opening title, which depicts a skeleton astride a horse, with the name of the film written in letters made of bones and the description "A super production . . . with Peggy Miller, Henry Mosle, & an all star cast." At the end of the reel, a single fragment of a second title card is found, indicating "PHOTOGRAPHY S. W. CHILDS JR. AND FIELD ASSISTANTS." The second artifact is a large, framed, handmade poster, again with bone lettering, focused around a photograph of three men in black cloaks and skull masks. "S. WINSTON CHILDS JR PRESENTS THE PURITY PLAYERS IN THE HORSEMEN OF DEATH." *Movie Makers* described the film when Childs donated a copy of the film to its collection:

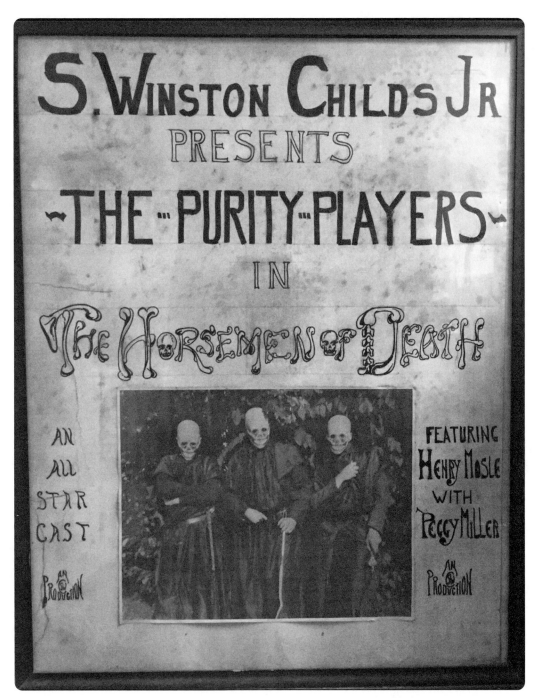

Figure 4. *The Horsemen of Death* (circa 1926) poster. Photograph by Brian Meacham.

The Horsemen of Death, 2000 ft., 16 mm., another permanent gift of Mr. Childs, further wins the gratitude of all who use the Library. A very early photoplay effort, it is a wild tale of wholesale vendetta led by a bereaved young man to avenge the gruesome but casual murder of his sweetheart. Friends and acquaintances join the awful band and a holocaust of horror ensues that will tighten the scalp of even the most blasé club projectionist.[24]

In 1927, Childs's senior year at Yale, the group tackled its final and most ambitious project: an adaptation of Henry Fielding's *Tom Jones*. Featuring a cast of more than thirty actors, the film was called by *Movie Makers* "the first amateur super-feature."[25] The ambitious production was filmed, according to the program for its premiere, in "private houses, in student's rooms, and the Memorial Quadrangle in Yale University; in a private residence in New York; and at a Country Seat at Norfolk in Connecticut." The filmmakers made much of the fact that the Purity Players' production was the first filmed adaptation of Fielding's novel, and a contemporaneous article in the *Yale Daily News* claimed that "this production will mark the first time that any of the major English novels of the Eighteenth Century has been adopted for the silver screen."[26] According to a 1927 issue of *Bell and Howell's Filmo Topics,* "it was shortly before the Easter recess that the college student seniors comprising the Purity Players conceived the plan of producing a motion picture."[27] The lengthy and somewhat troubled production was completed in June, just before the end of the academic year, and was cut down from fifteen reels to fourteen, with a running time of approximately two and a half hours. It was screened during commencement weekend to a packed house of 750 attendees at Yale's Sprague Hall and was described by faculty in the Yale English department as "splendid," "wonderfully spontaneous," and "one of the best things done at Yale in years."[28] In a letter to the editors of the *Yale Daily News* in 1951, Childs claimed that the film was well received and that "only two old ladies left the performance on June 12."[29] This opinion was not necessarily shared by all, however. In a 1971 interview with Jonas Mekas, the artist and filmmaker Jerome Hill, who played the roles of Mrs. Partridge and Mrs. Miller, in addition to designing costumes for the film, described it as "the worst film you've ever seen."[30] While it is perhaps unsurprising that, with hindsight, the acclaimed experimental and documentary filmmaker Hill disparaged his group's youthful efforts, it would be interesting to know whether he ever saw Childs's later, more experimental amateur films and what he might have thought of them.

Despite Childs's claim in the same 1951 letter to the *Yale Daily News* that "the original film of the picture is in the vault of the Yale library," the library held no copy of the film when a search was conducted in 2016. All fourteen reels of the film were eventually located within Hope Childs's donation.

Beyond the celebrated screening at Yale in June 1927, no evidence of further public screenings of the film has been found. Hope Childs, in a 2020 interview, mentioned that the family was "very proud that it had been made," and that single reels of the film were occasionally screened, but that "I was never a part of anybody sitting down to watch it all."[31] The film, made mostly by seniors and which premiered the weekend of their graduation from college, seems to have been designed to make a splash as a culmination of an intensive group effort, but with no consideration made for future screenings for those outside the filmmakers' circle.

After graduation from Yale, Childs's interest in film continued. In a May 1929 piece in *Movie Makers,* Childs, described as a "well-known amateur producer and travel film expert," is reported as the new, temporary manager of Home Film Libraries Inc., taking over from its founder, Orton F. Hicks.[32] Hicks had begun the company in 1927 as a way of offering "major studio-produced shorts to the developing 16mm home market."[33] Childs continued his affiliation with the company after it was renamed Films Incorporated in the mid-1930s and acquired by Eric Haight in May 1938.[34] In a 1952 notice in *Production Encyclopedia,* Childs is named chairman of the board of Films Inc., alongside Haight as president.[35] The two shared a long history; in fact, Eric Haight had starred as Partridge to Childs's Squire Western in Childs's production of *Tom Jones* twenty-five years before.

The Cynniewink Ciners

After Childs's graduation, he married Cynthia Cheney of Manchester, Connecticut.[36] Under the "Cynniewink" banner, they shared the work of directing, staging, and acting in their films, including *Riding the "Big Red" Aunts* (1929), *In the Leprous Hands of Lust* (1931), *I'd Be Delighted To!,* and *Seductio ad Absurdum.*

While some of the Cynniewink productions continued the earlier Purity Players tradition of imitating typical silent film genres, such as the western or the "white slavery" film, Childs also moved in a more experimental direction with his last two films.[37] His best-known production is *I'd Be Delighted To!,* a thirteen-minute short film that tells the story of a man and woman preparing for and enjoying a dinner date. As Childs described it in an article in *Movie Makers,* "I got the idea that it would be fun to film the action of some person's hand, say at a cocktail party. Upon this slender thread the light tinsel of *I'd Be Delighted To!* was hung."[38] Childs's camera focuses on the hands and feet of the film's protagonists; in fact, according to Hope Childs (and as evidenced by a handwritten label on one can containing a print of the film), the family referred to the film simply as

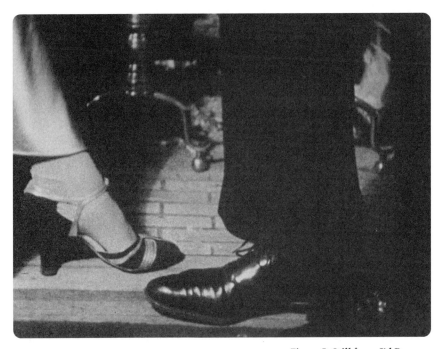

Figure 5. Still from *I'd Be Delighted To!* (1932). Courtesy Yale Film Archive.

"Hands and Feet," rather than by its more formal title. Bathing, dressing, greeting, eating, drinking, and relaxing after the meal are all shown through the movements of the hands and feet of the unnamed, unseen man and woman (as well as the man's maid, whose hands are seen preparing dinner in several shots).

Awarded an honorable mention alongside the *Movie Makers* "Ten Best" list for 1932, *I'd Be Delighted To!* received praise from the editorial staff of the magazine for being "that kind of production often planned but seldom made—a film story told entirely in closeups." The article went on to describe the film, made with Childs's "distinctly advanced amateur filming method," as "adroit, amusing and sophisticated."[39] As a result, Childs was invited by the magazine to write an article about using close-ups in amateur films. In it, Childs advocates for the inclusion of close-ups in home productions, offering that "it is amazingly easy to create, by shrewd selection, even a distinctly foreign atmosphere right in the home or backyard." He recalls,

> It was fun making the picture. It was fun filming the thousand and one incidents which go to make up such an evening—his hand lifting the telephone, her foot testing the temperature of the bath, his feet behind the shower curtain, her fingers deftly applying the lipstick, his hands wielding icepick, the maid's hands basting the chicken, her hand ringing the doorbell and so on through

the evening. It was all fun, but more important than that was the realization of the potential possibilities of this type of film treatment to supplement and lend color to all of one's pictures.[40]

The judges presiding over *American Cinematographer* magazine's "Amateur Movie Makers Contest of 1932," who included Joan Crawford, Cecil B. DeMille, Clark Gable, and Helen Hayes, also lauded Childs's film: "His photography, all of which was interior, was rated very high."[41] *I'd Be Delighted To!* was awarded third prize, which included his choice of "any standard Cooke telephoto lens for a Filmo camera" from Bell and Howell, which later featured Childs, holding his Filmo camera with its new lens, in an advertisement headlined "How to Win a Personal Movie Contest."[42]

And like *Movie Makers, American Cinematographer* invited Childs to write a piece for publication, this time about lighting for home movies. Childs opened his piece with a recollection of the production of *Tracks of Blood* with the Purity Players:

> In early days of home movies, before the advent of fast lenses, panchromatic film, and efficient incandescent light units, about the only practical method open to the amateur for indoor sequences in his productions was an outdoor set. Bristol board sets on the tennis court, or open porches furnished to resemble a living room, pantry, or whatever it might be, were essential if one was to get sufficient light. I well remember the "Silver Dollar Saloon" set which I built on our tennis court for one of my first productions, and the constant danger of showing the top of the set with tennis netting and trees in the background![43]

Childs also reflected on his most recent film:

> One of the shots I like best in I'D BE DELIGHTED TO is one of a hand picking up a stalk of asparagus at dinner. I held the camera on a level with the table, while the light came from over the diner's shoulder, throwing the top of the hand into strong relief. Yet the reflected light from the plate gave me all sorts of shadow contrasts, constantly changing as more or less light came through the fingers.

The film also won first prize from the French Federation of Amateur Cinema Clubs, awarded in Paris in December 1933, alongside films from France, Italy, Holland, Japan, and Yugoslavia. Through the Amateur Cinema League's "Club Film Library," screenings of the film were reported in *Movie Makers,* at local clubs in American cities like Kansas City and Indianapolis, and as far afield as Wimbledon, England, and Curaçao and Aruba in the Caribbean.[44]

The film continued to echo in the amateur cinema world in the coming years, with one amateur filmmaker proposing a film scenario in *American Cinematographer* in 1934, saying, "This picture can be made in the normal manner, or with the Lubitsch technique of 'I'd Be Delighted To!,' using only close-ups of feet and legs, hands and arms, etc."[45]

For a number of years, a copy of *I'd Be Delighted To!* has been available for viewing on the website of the East Anglian Film Archive as part of its Institute of Amateur Cinematographers Collection.[46] This transfer was the only work of S. W. Childs Jr. widely available and, outside the collection held by his family, the only evidence of his work available to the public. When the Yale Film Archive preserved the film from the best surviving elements in the S. W. Childs Jr. Collection in 2018, it became clear that the version available online was in fact incomplete, missing the six shots, totaling thirty-five seconds, that end the film.

Alongside the films themselves, Hope Childs's donation included a scrapbook assembled by her father-in-law that held the key to the story of this alternate version. C. J. VerHalen of *American Cinematographer* wrote to Childs, in a letter dated December 9, 1932, to congratulate him on his prize:

> The photography and lighting, as well as composition, was commented on very highly by the judges. The ending of your story, however, almost eliminated this picture. In showing this picture to the press, as well as the few public showings we have given it here, we have always stopped the picture before the ending. May we suggest that if you present this at any time in a public way as the prize winning picture that you edit one copy of it, so as to eliminate the scene which might be construed as questionable in its morals.

The cut version available online ends, before an end title card added later, with a close-up of the woman's shoes as she sits on the couch. In the uncut original version of the film, this shot continues on for another few seconds, followed by six more scenes: first, a shot of the fireplace, then a shot that shows both pairs of feet next to one another on the couch, after which she swings her feet up onto the couch, followed by his. The next shot shows him placing her dress on the arm of the couch, followed by one of his hand dropping his bow tie onto a side table, then one showing her slip dropping from an unseen hand onto the floor. Finally, we see her hand reaching for the light and turning it off, before the film fades to black, followed by Childs's original "The End" title. The Yale Film Archive preserved *I'd Be Delighted To!* in 2018 from the original reversal positive, including this "questionable" ending, and the 16mm preservation of the film premiered at the Orphan Film Symposium in New York, with a score by composer Stephen Horne, in April 2018.

While much is known about the making and reception of *I'd Be Delighted To!,* relatively little is known about its companion piece, another Cynniewink production called *Seductio ad Absurdum.* Cynthia Childs is credited with direction and continuity and also stars in the film, while S. W. Childs Jr. is credited with photography and special effects. The film tells another tale of a man and woman and a night out but, this time, the story takes the form of a vivid daydream. Cynthia Childs's character, disappointed that her husband doesn't seem to have remembered their anniversary, imagines she's having a romantic fling with a society gentleman, who takes her out to dinner, a fireworks display, and a Broadway show. The film features many close-ups reminiscent of *I'd Be Delighted To!* but doesn't restrict itself to hands and feet. Shot on Kodachrome color reversal stock, and with a sizable cast, the film feels like a natural progression from the earlier Cynniewink production. Among its many effects, the film employs direct address, flashback, double exposure, wipe edits using a rotating matte disk, and many of the close-up and lighting techniques Childs laid out in his two published articles. The Yale Film Archive preserved *Seductio ad Absurdum* from the reversal original in 2019. With another score composed and performed by Stephen Horne, a new print of the film was premiered at the Northeast Historic Film Summer Symposium in 2019, bringing full circle the story of the Childs Collection, back to the archive where it was first uncovered by Ryan Shand four years earlier.

CONCLUSION

Advocacy around amateur film's importance as a creative record of time and place, and increased awareness of its fragility as an often unique carrier of this history, has meant that many film collections held by filmmakers and their families have been placed in the care of film archives around the world. But despite this move to archives, countless important film collections are still out there, stored in family attics and closets, often undervalued or overlooked by those who care for them. Archivists are often faced with questions like "Why would you want those films?" or "Are you sure those would be interesting to someone else?" when inquiring about home movies and amateur films, and filmmakers' children and grandchildren might be surprised to learn about the historical and cultural value to be found in their family's films.

By contextualizing the films of S. W. and Cynthia Childs in the larger histories of filmmaking at Yale, early 16mm student filmmaking in the United States, and the global popularity of amateur film production in the 1930s and 1940s, the importance of the Childs Collection is clear. As prolific and oft cited as Childs and his films were, though, without the initial research inquiry from Ryan Shand, the Childses' body of work might never have been acquired for preservation. And without the assertion to the Childs family that these films were important enough to hold on to, donate, and work with the Yale Film Archive to properly catalog, who knows what might have become of them? The fact that the family had a somewhat unique name, and was still connected to the university, made locating them fairly simple; but when we learned about the extent of Childs's work, and the relative fame he and the Purity Players had achieved in their day, we were surprised that this important collection had not been acquired for archival preservation sooner.[47]

Upon reflection of this case study, it appears that there are two main ways to research amateur films. Either you can identify amateur films that are already part of an archival collection and then try to source relevant contextual material, or you can consult archival paper records for details of amateur films that have been made but are not currently held by archives. In the example summarized here, we started with the film and then went searching for contextual information. However, as the collaboration developed, it became necessary to adopt the second approach, which is inherently more collaborative. Historians can form partnerships with archives in an attempt to locate amateur films, or archives could invite historians to aid their acquisition processes.[48] Indeed, Edmonds has previously suggested that "if researchers could produce a list of amateur fiction films, filmmakers and cine clubs that have appeared in the written discourse, archivists would be able to use this to track down canonical amateur fiction films."[49] These partnerships between archivists and scholars could develop in many ways. For example, if other archivists and scholars were similarly interested in locating amateur films made by students, then a potentially useful partnership could be formed with university alumni offices, which might be able to help with contacting the families of former filmmakers.

This research into early amateur fiction films developed out of what initially seemed to be the identification of an idiosyncratic feature film made by students. However, in 2019, an article was published on a feature-length amateur fiction film made in 1929.[50] Interestingly, this case study was also a research collaboration, on this occasion between a film historian and a university librarian. Our study similarly drew on a range of newspaper and magazine sources, which we utilized to understand amateur film culture of the 1920s. Reflecting on their research methodologies, Aronson and Peterson noted,

> Excavating the myriad histories of student filmmaking requires different kinds of detective work and labor than traditional film research methods, and while sources like college newspapers can present significant challenges to access, as evident in this particular film's history, they offer the potential to provide meaningful context and insight into the production.[51]

The emergence of a comparable case study on campus-based filmmaking at the University of Oregon, at around the same time as ours, suggests that research on early amateur fiction films is becoming increasingly possible, at least partly as a result of newly available access to digitized print sources.

In this article, we made a case for the importance of student filmmaking to the early history of amateur cinema. Of course, this research has primarily focused on the United Kingdom and the United States but, in his *Photoplay* article, Frederick James Smith claimed that "amateur film work began to be taken up by universities all over the world."[52] Therefore our wider question to international film archivists and historians is, what does the early history of campus cine-clubs look like in other countries? We suggest that archivists and historians could play an active role in developing new histories of early amateur filmmaking in other national contexts.

Brian Meacham is managing archivist at the Yale Film Archive, where he has overseen the film collection since 2013. He is responsible for acquiring, inspecting, and cataloging the archive's film collection and has supervised the preservation of more than twenty-five films in the collection. He received a certificate in film preservation from the L. Jeffrey Selznick School of Film Preservation at the George Eastman Museum in 2006 and worked as public access coordinator and subsequently short film preservationist at the Academy Film Archive from 2006 to 2013. He teaches a course on the film archive for the Yale Film and Media Studies graduate program and researches the cultural and technological history of the analog photobooth, as well as the ways in which filmmakers and cinephiles document their moviegoing histories.

Ryan Shand, PhD, is a research manager at Queen Mary University of London. He completed his PhD in film and television studies at the University of Glasgow. Ryan was previously a postdoctoral researcher on Arts and Humanities Research Council–funded projects at the University of Liverpool and the University of Glasgow. He contributed chapters to the anthologies *Locating the Moving Image* (2014), *Materializing Memories* (2018), and **British Art Cinema** (2019). His article publications have appeared in *The Moving Image, Leisure Studies,* and the *Film Education Journal.* Ryan is also the coeditor of *Small-Gauge Storytelling: Discovering the Amateur Fiction Film* (2013).

NOTES

1. This project, titled "Children and Amateur Media in Scotland," was based at the University of Glasgow between 2010 and 2014. It was funded by the Arts and Humanities Research Council.
2. Marjorie Agnes Lovell Burgess, *The Amateur Ciné Movement: A Popular Account of Its Development in Great Britain* (London: Sampson, 1932), 4–5.
3. Heather Norris Nicholson, *Amateur Film: Meaning and Practice, 1927–77* (Manchester, U.K.: Manchester University Press, 2012), 56.
4. https://www.youtube.com/watch?v=dIWfr5ptzEM.
5. Guy Edmonds, "Historical, Aesthetic, Cultural: The Problematical Value of Amateur Cine Fiction," in *Small-Gauge Storytelling: Discovering the Amateur Fiction Film,* ed. Ryan Shand and Ian Craven (Edinburgh: Edinburgh University Press, 2013), 34.
6. This fellowship honors the legacy of the Canadian film archivist William O'Farrell, "a long time advocate for amateur and nontheatrical film collections": https://oldfilm.org/content/william-s-ofarrell-fellowship.
7. These funds were provided by the Creative Futures Institute, based at the University of the West of Scotland.
8. Adrian Brunel, *Filmcraft: The Art of Picture Production* (London: George Newnes, 1935).
9. Brunel, 235.
10. Adrian Brunel, *Nice Work: The Story of Thirty Years in British Film Production* (London: Forbes Robertson, 1949), and Brunel, *Film Production* (London: Newnes, 1936).

11. "Manchester Movies," *Movie Makers* 3, no. 6 (1928): 391.

12. Media History Digital Library: https://mediahistoryproject.org/.

13. Frederick James Smith, "Amateur Movies: Photoplay's Contest Closes with Many Interesting Entries," *Photoplay* 35, no. 6 (1929): 72.

14. Smith, 72.

15. This information on the introduction of 16mm safety film is included in the "Chronology" appendix of the following edited collection: Ian Craven, ed., *Movies on Home Ground: Explorations in Amateur Cinema* (Newcastle upon Tyne, U.K.: Cambridge Scholars, 2009), 328.

16. "Hollywood at Harkness: Yale Students Are First to Film Famous Novel," *Amateur Movie Maker* 2, no. 8 (1927): 48.

17. *Movie Makers* 5, no. 9 (1930): 569. It is currently unclear what happened to the Amateur Cinema League's Club Film Library following the league's incorporation into the Photographic Society of America and, later, the American Motion Picture Society. In 2003, Alan D. Kattelle wrote that at some point, "award-winning films were ultimately returned to their makers. Many of the winning films have been lost, particularly those of the first two decades of the League." Kattelle, "The Amateur Cinema League and Its Films," *Film History* 15, no. 2 (2003): 242.

18. Yale Daily News Historical Archive: http://digital.library.yale.edu/cdm/landingpage/collection/yale-ydn.

19. "Closeups and Swaps," *Amateur Movie Makers* 2, no. 7 (1927): 31.

20. "Closeups and Swaps," 31.

21. Benjamin Spock and S. W. Childs Jr. were brothers-in-law; Spock married Jane Cheney in 1927 and, two years later, Childs married Jane's sister Cynthia Cheney.

22. "Closeups and Swaps," 31.

23. "Closeups and Swaps," 31.

24. Arthur L. Gale, "Amateur Clubs," *Movie Makers* 5, no. 9 (1930): 569.

25. Gale, 569.

26. "Tickets for Tom Jones to Go on Sale To-Day," *Yale Daily News* 50, no. 192 (1927): 1.

27. "Yale Seniors Put 'Tom Jones' to Screen," *Filmo Topics* 3, no. 8 (1927): 1.

28. "Hollywood at Harkness," 48.

29. S. Winston Childs Jr., "This First Flick Business," *Yale Daily News* 73, no. 103 (1951): 2.

30. Jonas Mekas, "An Interview with Jerome Hill, September 5, 1971, New York. Interviewer: Jonas Mekas," *Film Culture* 56–57 (1973): 3–17.

31. "Treasures from the Yale Film Archive Presents: The S. W. Childs, Jr. Collection," Vimeo, 37:01, September 21, 2020, https://vimeo.com/460206792.

32. "News of the Industry," *Movie Makers* 4, no. 5 (1929): 335.

33. Geoff Alexander, *Academic Films for the Classroom: A History* (Jefferson, N.C.: McFarland, 2010), 99.

34. Anthony Slide, *The New Historical Dictionary of the American Film Industry* (Abingdon, U.K.: Routledge, 2014), 74.

35. *Production Encyclopedia* (Hollywood, Calif.: Hollywood Reporter, 1952), 668.

36. While Childs's Yale connections and film story are well known, Cynthia

Cheney's family history had a small film connection as well: the roots of the Cheneys in the United States stretch back to the 1600s and include Ward, Frank, and Rush Cheney, who founded Cheney Brothers silk manufacturing in the 1800s. The company received credits for providing silks in at least six Warner Bros./First National Films in 1932–33, including *I Am a Fugitive from a Chain Gang* and *42nd Street*.

37. For more information on so-called white slavery films, see Shelley Stamp Lindsey, "Wages and Sin: Traffic in Souls and the White Slavery Scare," *Persistence of Vision*, no. 9 (1991): 90–102.

38. S. Winston Childs Jr., "The Closeup's the Thing," *Movie Makers* 8, no. 2 (1933): 65.

39. "The Ten Best," *Movie Makers* 8, no. 12 (1932): 537.

40. Childs, "Closeup's the Thing," 65.

41. "More than 200 Compete for Amateur Prizes," *American Cinematographer* 8, no. 8 (1932): 7.

42. "How to Win a Personal Movie Contest," *American Cinematographer* 12, no. 10 (1933): 2.

43. S. W. Childs Jr., "Lighting for Home Movies," *American Cinematographer* 12, no. 10 (1933): 23.

44. "Film Exchange Methods," *Movie Makers* 5, no. 6 (1930): 374.

45. K. G. Stephens, "Backyard Movies," *American Cinematographer* 15, no. 1 (1934): 37.

46. *I'd Be Delighted To!* (1934), East Anglian Film Archive, catalog no. 3436, http://eafa.org.uk/work/?id=1025785.

47. The Purity Players are mentioned in the "Historical Background" opening section of Kattelle's "Amateur Cinema League," 238.

48. A number of academic research projects have been conducted in partnership with film archives but, as far as we are aware, almost all of them focused on researching existing archival collections, rather than aiming to expand the amateur film collections of the archive partner. However, the "Children and Amateur Media in Scotland" project at the University of Glasgow, from 2010 to 2014, sought to acquire amateur films and videos made in Scotland from 1970 to 2010. The project budget included funds to cover the curator's salary during a period of secondment, when the project focused entirely on new acquisitions to the archive.

49. Edmonds, "Historical, Aesthetic, Cultural," 51–52.

50. Michael Aronson and Elizabeth Peterson, "'Planned, Plotted, Played, Pictured by Students': The Ambitious Amateurs of *Ed's Coed* (1929)," *Film History* 31, no. 2 (2019): 60–88.

51. Aronson and Peterson, 84.

52. Smith, "Amateur Movies," 72.

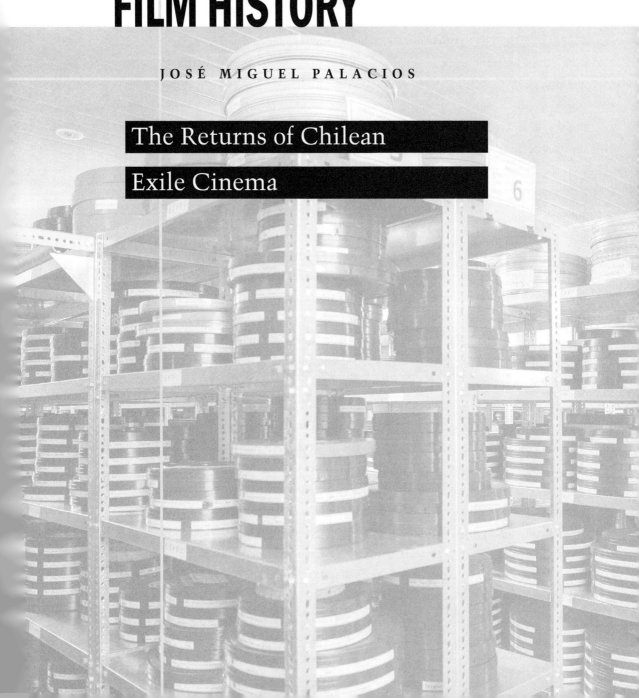

EXILE, ARCHIVES, AND TRANSNATIONAL FILM HISTORY

JOSÉ MIGUEL PALACIOS

The Returns of Chilean

Exile Cinema

This article stems from a research project that sought to determine the presence of 16mm, 35mm, and other filmic materials belonging to Chilean exile cinema in different archives throughout the world and to establish a catalog of the exile films that had returned to Chilean institutions, studying the means by which this return had taken place.[1] A detailed report on archival considerations relevant to this diasporic corpus constitutes the bulk of what follows, examining issues of access, location, cataloging, institutional histories, curatorial practices, funding, cultural and political contexts, infrastructures, and online platforms. As these issues configure the basis of the material conditions that enable scholars to do historical research, the article deals with another set of problems that explore the broader relations between exile, the archive, and the writing of transnational film histories. Following Nataša Ďurovičová, I am interested in transnationalism's capacity to revise standard historiographic narratives, not as an aggregate of distinct national film histories, but as a spatial lens through which to map how cinema moves through borders of various kinds.[2] Exilic cinemas imply a specific variant of transnationalism in that they live in the spaces *in between* nations. My larger purpose is thus to reflect on the challenges that exile, as a cultural and political experience of forced displacement, and exile cinema, as a mode of transnational media that inhabits a liminal space, raise for the archive. In doing so, this article contributes to an emerging scholarship that critiques the national paradigm dominating most film archives and that calls attention to power imbalances in global archival networks.[3]

After the 1973 military coup that put an end to the socialist government of Salvador Allende, more than two hundred thousand Chileans were forced into exile.[4] Owing to the politicized nature of their filmic practice, usually associated with the radical energy of the New Latin American cinema movement, Chilean filmmakers were part of this wave of displacement. In exile, they made more than two hundred short-, medium-, and feature-length fiction films, documentaries, animations, videos, and works for television in countries as varied as Brazil, Cuba, Canada, Finland, France, Germany (East and West), Mexico, Mozambique, Romania, Spain, Sweden, the United States, the Soviet Union, and Venezuela.[5] Most films denounced the crimes of the dictatorship or focused on exile itself as a social and psychological process. But in other cases, directors purposefully tried to do away with all explicit ties connecting them to Chile. As Zuzana M. Pick recognized, Chilean exile cinema never constituted a movement in the programmatic sense of the term.[6] Besides a wide thematic and aesthetic range, Chilean exile cinema is the result of a variety of modes of production found by filmmakers in the different cultural and political contexts in which they worked, including state studios, independent productions, television networks, national film institutes or agencies, film schools, and artisanal and collective modes of filmmaking.[7]

Even if the bulk of this corpus coincides with the temporal frame of the military dictatorship led by Augusto Pinochet, Chilean exile cinema is not circumscribed to this period. Various directors never returned to the country after the end of the military rule; many kept on making films that dealt explicitly with the condition of exile; and several filmmakers of the "second generation," the children of the diaspora, are nowadays producing films about the lasting effects of exile and return on their lives.[8] For these motives, Chilean exile cinema remains an ongoing cultural phenomenon. But there is yet another reason to claim that Chilean exile cinema does not belong to the past. Since the mid-2000s, part of this corpus has begun its return to Chilean institutions—Cineteca Nacional de Chile, Cineteca de la Universidad de Chile, Museo de la Memoria y los Derechos Humanos, and Archivo Ruiz-Sarmiento—through mechanisms like donations by filmmakers, the signing of international cooperation agreements, and the programming of special retrospectives. This last instrument is relevant because return cannot be reduced to the acts of depositing and storing films in an archive. In 2013, I was part of a team of six scholars who programmed a series called *Nomadías* (Nomadisms) for the twentieth edition of the Valdivia International Film Festival in 2013. The series was devoted to three women filmmakers in exile, Marilú Mallet, Valeria Sarmiento, and Angelina Vázquez, whose work in Canada, France, and Finland remained largely unknown in Chile. The program involved bringing digital files of titles, such as *La femme au foyer* (Valeria Sarmiento, France, 1976), that had never been screened in Chile and of which no local archive held copies. In a round panel held during the retrospective, director Angelina Vázquez claimed, "I returned in 1993, but my films have never returned."[9] Since she herself had deposited most of her films in Cineteca Nacional de Chile a few years before the retrospective, by this she could only mean one thing: *my films are invisible.* Paraphrasing Hamid Naficy, Vázquez seemed to be saying that "an exile cinema may return, yet still not fully arrive."[10] When I speak of return, then, I am also talking about access and visibility. Exhibiting Chilean exile films in their theaters and loaning them for series organized by other institutions and festivals have been the main means used by the four aforementioned archives and museums to bring this diasporic corpus closer to Chilean audiences, a significant goal considering that most exile films never received theatrical distribution in Chile and were never programmed on national television. In recent years, access has increased thanks to digitization projects and the inclusion of some of these films in the online platforms Cineteca Nacional Online (by Cineteca Nacional de Chile) and Cineteca Virtual (by Cineteca de la Universidad de Chile).

Because most exile films remain unseen by Chilean audiences and scholars, the returns of Chilean exile cinema have relevant implications for understanding the role of this corpus in national film history and for situating its material and symbolic function in the country almost thirty years after the end of the dictatorship.[11] This larger phenomenon is what I mean by "archival returns"—the process that has brought prints and copies of exile films to Chilean archives and museums, as well as the cultural demands, historical narratives, and memory debates activated by that process. *Return* is a tricky word to use in this archival context, and I shall soon explain why it is in fact the appropriate term in detriment of the more commonly used *film repatriation*. For the moment, it will suffice to say that exile and return are mutually defining concepts: one cannot be understood without the other. In fact, to speak of archival returns is also to speak of what remains in exile. For the most part, Chilean exile films continue to be safeguarded in multiple archives across different continents. In an evocative phrase, Elizabeth Ramírez-Soto calls this dispersion the "scattered body" of Chilean exile cinema.[12] If Chilean exile cinema is a corpus, its parts are to be found in all corners of the world and in different kinds of archives.

In what follows, I acknowledge such a plurality by discussing a range of archives that currently store Chilean exile cinema and therefore play a significant role in the histories that can be written about it. But the organizations that will be discussed herein are not homogeneous, as there are great differences between the highly professional and specialized archives in countries like France or Sweden and the "imperfect archives" of Latin America—those "orphans of the moving image archival infrastructure," as Janet Ceja Alcalá called them.[13] The main questions that lurk throughout this article are therefore political more than technological. Competing discourses of cultural heritage and trans/national film history are at stake in the archival returns of Chilean exile cinema. These stakes derive from the particular nature of exile cinemas, which always bear the mark of the "interstitial," as described by Hamid Naficy, a state of ongoing in-betweenness.[14] Exile implies being forever caught in the ambiguous zone that lies between two governing bodies, those of the country of origin and those of the host society. Although exile films share several features of what has been variously called "multicultural," "intercultural," "transnational," and "accented" cinemas, and though all of them critique hegemonic modes of understanding the national, exile cinemas defy any sense of proper emplacement.[15] The interstitiality of exile points to a fundamental aspect of the term *displacement*: being *out* of place, regardless of where exile subjects and cultural artifacts reside. This is why I insist on speaking of "Chilean exile cinema" as opposed to Chilean cinema "in" exile, as most scholars and critics do.[16] The former concept alludes to a cinema both *in* and *about* exile; produces an intertwining of "exile cinema" with the historical development of the "Chilean exile" experience; and emphasizes the inherent instability of the condition of exile, irreducible to a single position.

This article is therefore devoted to the following paradox: although the archival presence of a film demands a specific positionality, no particular archival location can account for the multiplicity of geographic and cultural displacements evidenced by exile cinemas.

RETURN; OR, THE CULTURAL POLITICS OF REPATRIATION

Exile destabilizes what Caroline Frick has described as the logic that ties the discourse of cultural heritage to the nation as "a particular level of authority and power."[17] Even if film archives have regularly collected "far more than their own countries' film productions," as Adelheid Heftberger reminds us, the symbolic and material power of the national dominates the policies and practices of most archival institutions—especially those that are called "national" film archives and cinematheques, which produce an indissoluble triad between national heritage, national film history, and the national archive.[18] In the world of museums and archives, discourses of repatriation have challenged the traditional understanding of heritage based on notions of possession and exclusivity, but they do not necessarily challenge the national paradigm within which archives work.[19] According to Paolo Cherchi Usai, the narrow and most frequently used definition of repatriation understands it as "the physical transfer of prints from one archive to the other on the basis of their nationality."[20] Etymologically, the Latin root *patria* adds enormous weight to the kinds of exchanges present in repatriation projects, tied as they are to postwar and postcolonial contexts, as well as to other situations of cultural and political violence.[21] Regardless of the specificity of the case, repatriation is fundamentally about nationhood, heritage, and belonging.

But where do exile films belong? And what (national) institutions can claim a right to them? Liminality is at the heart of the exile condition and is the main reason why repatriation is problematic as concept and as practice for dealing with exilic cultural production. It is true that many films can be found in archives that are located in countries that differ from the territory of their production or from the nationality of their filmmakers, and it is also true that the presence of an exile print in a particular archive responds to a series of circumstances that are also shared by nonexile films, such as coproduction agreements, festival programming, market sales, and dubbing or subtitling of prints for specific international territories. However, Chilean exile cinema poses a specific kind of "anomaly" for the film archive for two main reasons.[22] One refers to the political nature of exile as an experience of forced displacement, coupled with the explicit political project of a cinema of resistance against the dictatorship. In this regard, the travels and movements of exile prints often respond to the intricacies of a circulatory network of transnational solidarities with the Chilean people, where a range of actors that normally fall under the cracks of the archive intervene: solidarity committees, exile communities, embassies and consulates, labor organizations, film clubs, and so on. The second reason speaks to the question of belonging. If archival examples of war and postcolonial contexts configure a situation in which a work of art, material artifact, or film print *from* a particular nation has been usurped by a foreign power, in the case of exile cinemas, that *from* remains ambiguous. Exile prints belong simultaneously *here* and *there*. Consider *Il n'y a pas d'oubli* (Rodrigo González, Marilú Mallet, and Jorge Fajardo, 1975), a film about the exile experience made by three Chilean exile directors in Canada; produced by the National Film Board with a Canadian crew and a mix of Canadian and Chilean actors (including exiles playing a version of themselves); and spoken in Spanish, French, and English. The film is *undoubtedly* Canadian; however, even if it has never enjoyed a theatrical release or television broadcast in Chile, and even if no Chilean archive holds a print or digital file of it, *Il n'y a pas d'oubli,* for its portrayal of an emerging exilic community, bears an indelible bond with Chile, that country where it was not made, where it has not been shown, and where it is not safeguarded.

If a sense of belonging is shared by different nations, how to speak of repatriation for exile cinemas? What right would a Chilean archive claim for holding a print of *Il n'y a pas d'oubli* as part of its collection? An alternative is raised by Cherchi Usai, for whom the safeguarding of "moral rights" presupposes a different repatriation scheme.[23] Arguing that "nationality is not necessarily a criterion for repatriation" allows for a much broader understanding of the repatriation process: "returning cinematic works to their community of origin for the purposes of collection development, preservation, public dissemination, or for the protection of the community's cultural interests."[24] This definition could apply to the case of Chilean exile cinema, if it were clear that this cinema responded to the "community's cultural interests." But what community is invoked here? With repatriation, we arrive at a dead end, because it is impossible to answer this question without falling back on a national (Chilean) or political allegiance (opponents to the dictatorship).

I prefer to speak of archival returns because return is the concept that connects the films as a form of cultural heritage, even as a form of cultural exchange property, with the specific historical condition that produced them—exile. The notion of archival returns points to the limitations of the institution of the archive when dealing with both exile as a cultural phenomenon and exile cinema as a fundamentally transnational corpus. Archival safeguarding and preservation demand a precise location, a fixed positionality that does not reflect the core characteristics of transnationalism and exile: connectedness, mobility, and in-betweenness. The idea of an archival return does not solve these limitations; it could even be said that it reinforces them, because return presupposes the homeland, a national site of origin, as the final destination for a cultural object that belongs to a place that is different from the one where it was produced. Most importantly, even if it does not do away with the weight of nationhood, the concept of archival returns charges the operation of cultural transfer and exchange with a sense of historical restitution.

Returns from exile participate from an institutional and political landscape that negotiates the writing of transnational film history and the production of memories of the dictatorship. Following Kirsten Weld in her understanding of archives as "instruments of political action" and "enablers of gaze and desire," I want to claim that the archival returns of Chilean exile cinema activate a triple desire.[25] First, they enable a desire for cultural and historical recognition: by returning to Chilean archives, it is acknowledged that these exile films belong *there,* where they had never resided in the first place. Second, they enable a desire for completion: the attempt to restore unity and continuity to Chilean cinema. As Paulo Antonio Paranaguá, Gastón Ancelovici, and Zuzana M. Pick respectively claimed, this was a cinema "split in two streams," divided between the films produced in exile and those that had been made in Chile under the dictatorship.[26] And third, they enable a desire for bearing witness, for acting as testimonies to the experience of exile—the desire to activate individual and collective memories of exile.

THE SCATTERED BODY OF EXILE

When one wishes to find the traces of Chilean exile cinema in international archives, the vastness of the corpus emerges as the first limitation. The most complete catalog to date was elaborated by Pick with materials gathered by herself and Cinemateca Chilena en el Exilio (more on this organization in the next section). Published in the U.S.-based exile journal *Literatura Chilena: Creación y Crítica* in 1984, this filmography lists 176 titles and covers the first decade of exilic production (1973–83).[27] Twenty years later, one of the first research projects undertaken by Cineteca Nacional de Chile soon after its founding in 2006 sought to find Chilean filmic materials in foreign archives "and, whenever possible, to obtain copies and repatriate them."[28] However, exile did not constitute its exclusive focus. Because there was no proper national film archive in the country, the research team also looked for materials produced in Chile prior to the coup and after 1990, plus films and newsreels made by foreigners in Chile, regardless of their date. Published in 2008, the concluding report acknowledged great difficulties in accomplishing the research task with regard to exilic production in particular. The main reasons cited were the dispersion in too many international archives, the diversity of film and video materials, and the lack of a detailed filmography.[29] The results were thus insufficient in the specific case of exile cinema, and the findings included several errors and imprecisions with regard to exile titles, the particular gauge of safeguarded materials, and the quantity of extant prints. Using these two catalogs as a starting point, the research I have conducted in person between 2018 and 2019 in archives located in Canada, Chile, France, Germany, Mexico, Spain, Sweden, and the United States—plus the revision of the searchable online catalogs of various other international archives— allows me to estimate a total of more than 230 Chilean exile films.[30]

Even if online archival databases have made the task easier, most of the difficul- ties listed in the 2008 report elaborated by Cineteca Nacional de Chile still persist. The second challenge I want to highlight is connected to the variety of modes of production and circulation of Chilean exile cinema. Some works were made for television but were never broadcast; several films played in festivals but received limited theatrical distri- bution afterward; and while an important number of Chilean exile films had production and distribution companies behind them, for the most part, these do not exist today (which is a problem when seeking rights and permissions to screen the films). It must be noted as well that a number of Chilean exile films now appear to be lost, or at least, they are yet to be found.[31] Because they were made in the margins of film industries and with little or no institutional support, these films were not deposited in any archive and were therefore not subject to their control and protection. As Beatriz Tadeo Fuica and Julieta Keldjian note, this was not an uncommon fate for many Latin American films in the 1970s and 1980s.[32] The last challenge is the physical dispersal itself, what Elizabeth Ramírez-Soto calls the "scattered body" of Chilean exile cinema in a metaphor that borrows the title from one of Raúl Ruiz's first films in exile, produced for the German television channel ZDF in 1975—*El cuerpo repartido y el mundo al revés* (Scattered body and the world upside down; also known as *Utopía*).[33]

The vast majority of 16mm and 35mm viewing prints, copies, original negatives, sound elements, U-matic and VHS tapes, and other filmic materials corresponding to Chilean exile cinema are currently stored in national film archives and cinematheques, museums, production companies, television archives, university libraries, archives of political parties, and labor archives throughout the world—evidence of the geographic dispersion suffered by their makers and of the very different industrial conditions under which Chilean directors worked.[34]

Archives that escape the category of the national cinematheque also constitute precious sources for locating marginal objects that generally fall under the label of the "orphan" film, understood here in the broad sense of "rare, unique or neglected films."[35] Chilean exile films that can be considered orphans include short audiovisual experiments made for television, such as *J'ai rencontré l'arbre à pain,* made by Valeria Sarmiento for the *Botaniques* series broadcast by Antenne 2 on September 5, 1982, and currently stored in France's Institut national de l'audiovisuel (INA); student films like *Margarita* (1978), made by José Echeverría while enrolled in the Department of Drama at Bristol University and now safeguarded in the British Film Institute; and other cinematic works that were made in an artisanal mode of production. Even if many of these titles are currently safeguarded in archives, they all share an orphanhood that is both material (damaged reels or unique prints that cannot be screened) and conceptual (unseen or forgotten works that have not been written into any kind of film history).[36]

Special collections managed by universities also hold a range of Chilean exile titles. After giving a series of talks at Duke University in 1994, Raúl Ruiz donated several film and video materials to Duke University Libraries in 1996.[37] Besides safeguarding 16mm prints of rare titles like *Viaggio clandestine—Vite di santi e di peccatori* (1994), the Raúl Ruiz Film and Videotape Collection, 1960–1996 is especially valuable for its holdings of work prints together with original sound elements and picture negatives. Materials found in the Duke collection were instrumental for the posthumous completion of *La telenovela errante* (The wandering soap opera), shot by Ruiz in 1990 but finished by Valeria Sarmiento and a small team of collaborators in 2017.[38]

In accordance with the significant role played by Chile's history in the political imagination of the Left during the 1970s and 1980s, several archives of political parties and labor groups store Chilean exile films in their collections. The 16mm prints of a film like *El color de la sangre no se olvida* (1974), made collectively by members of the Movement of Revolutionary Left party in homage to their assassinated leader Miguel Enríquez, are simultaneously held in the vaults of Fondazione Archivio Audiovisivo del Movimento Operaio e Democratico in Rome and in the International Institute of Social History in Amsterdam.[39] In the latter case, the film is part of the Cineclub Vrijheidsfilms, a rich collection with plenty of political documentaries from what was then called the Third World.[40] This collection evidences the extent to which politically oriented Chilean exile films traveled worldwide through alternative distribution networks run by cine-clubs and other associations, such as community groups and political parties. A special archive in this regard is Arsenal–Institut für Film und Videokunst in Berlin, then called "Friends of the German Cinematheque," which holds 16mm political documentaries made during Allende's government, several U-matic tapes that give an account of the prolific video scene in Chile throughout the 1980s, and 16mm and 35mm prints of at least seventeen Chilean exile films (Figure 1).[41]

National cinematheques and film archives, however, store the majority of Chilean exile titles, especially feature-length fiction films and documentaries. For example, the Swedish Film Institute (SFI) safeguards 16mm distribution prints of the internationalist solidarity documentary *Sången lever generaler* (Claudio Sapiaín, 1975), among others.[42] Organizations that function as national institutes in addition to their role as archives acted on several occasions as main commissioners, producers, or coproducers of Chilean exile films. This is why, for instance, SFI holds 35mm distribution prints plus original negatives and sound elements for *Prisioneros desaparecidos* (Sergio Castilla, 1979), a coproduction between SFI and Cuba's Instituto Cubano del Arte e Industria Cinematográficos (ICAIC).[43] In plenty of other instances, Chilean exile titles entered the collections of national cinematheques because they were programmed in their regular seasons or as part of special series. Filmoteca Española, for example, safeguards 35mm prints for more than ten films made by Miguel Littin, Raúl Ruiz, and Valeria Sarmiento that were once programmed there and, subsequently, remained in the archive.[44]

RETURNING TO CHILEAN ARCHIVES

This section analyzes the presence of Chilean exile films in the collections of four institutions—Cineteca Nacional de Chile, Cineteca de la Universidad de Chile, Museo de la Memoria y los Derechos Humanos, and Archivo Ruiz-Sarmiento. While these are not the sole film archives in the country, they have acted as key players in the return of Chilean exile cinema.[45] I want to focus here on the various mechanisms by which these four archives and museums have obtained 16mm and 35mm prints, videos, and digital files of this exilic corpus, as well as paper-based documentation relevant for the scholarly study of Chilean exile cinema.[46] A brief discussion of the nature of these institutions is necessary, because the approach each of them has taken toward safeguarding and presenting Chilean exile films can be explained to a large degree by their different histories, missions, archival practices, systems of governance, and sources of funding. As scholars have argued with regard to the Latin American archival scene, these last two features are not innocent, as they "determine the cultural policies of the institutions."[47] More broadly, all Chilean and Latin American archives share at least one common characteristic according to Maria Rita Galvão's famous 2006 report: "instability."[48] This instability is marked by a sense of ongoing financial precarity and a complicated relation with the state, which renders "archival preservation fragmentary and politically fraught."[49]

Figure 1. A rare 16mm print of *Metamorfosis del jefe de la policía política* (Helvio Soto, 1973), part of the film collection of the Arsenal–Institut für Film und Videokunst in Berlin.

Often, nonetheless, heads of archives reclaim this lack of resources, as it allows them to question what the First World regards as universal practices of preservation. The poverty of Chilean and Latin American archives is the most evident face of a profound imbalance between North and South that is not merely infrastructural; rather, the imbalance suggests that different archival institutional cultures might be created to respond to specific political and historical contexts.[50]

Archivo Ruiz-Sarmiento developed from the Art Institute of the private university Pontificia Universidad Católica de Valparaíso. It was founded in 2013, two years after Ruiz's death, as an homage to Chile's most important director, someone who had taught cinema between 1969 and 1972 in the same university department that now houses the archive.[51] Its mission concentrates on safeguarding the work of exile directors Raúl Ruiz and Valeria Sarmiento, who were married and developed intertwined careers as they collaborated in most of their films.[52] Limited to two filmmakers, this archive is thus much more restricted than the organizations that will be discussed herein. Although it possesses some DVD copies for on-site consultation, it cannot be considered a film archive, properly speaking. Its focus is placed on manuscript and iconographic documentation donated by Sarmiento—seventy boxes containing unfinished projects, correspondence, press clippings and dossiers, photographs, screenplays, budgets, grant proposals, and so on (Figure 2). An official catalog following international standards of classification was completed in 2020 and should soon be uploaded to the archive's website.[53] The physical location and overall mission of this institution resemble the rare manuscript section of a university library (Cuneo had the Beckett Collection at the University of Reading in the United Kingdom as a model).[54] But there is an important difference: Archivo Ruiz-Sarmiento is run without overstressing the usual gateways and protocols that archives and libraries follow to guarantee the preservation of documents. This institution privileges access above anything else, and Cuneo has emphasized a vision of the archive as a sort of "bookstore," where scholars "come in and chat" and generate knowledge through collaborative conversations.[55] It is important to mention, as well, another relevant foreign organization with regard to Archivo Ruiz-Sarmiento: the Institut Mémoires de l'édition contemporaine (IMEC), located outside of Caen, France. IMEC has housed forty-two archival boxes of Ruiz documents since 2012.[56] Soon after the creation of Archivo Ruiz-Sarmiento in Chile, Cuneo and IMEC's director agreed on an instrument of cooperation, centered on the duplication of each institution's documentary holdings, which was in the end never implemented, as it placed an impossible financial burden on the Chilean institution. This fact, together with the abysmal disparity in terms of physical settings—a very small university library room versus a monumental abbey—points to the already mentioned imbalance between European and Latin American archives. Regardless, Archivo Ruiz-Sarmiento has developed a fundamental role in bringing attention to a vast array of documentation that is allowing local scholars—for whom travel and access to European archives are more difficult—to produce new primary source research on this couple of filmmakers.

The next university archive I will discuss has a much longer and complicated history. Founded in 1961, Cineteca de la Universidad de Chile became the first public film archive in the country. Its development has been closely entangled with the rise of political cinemas in Chile, especially through the university's Centro de Cine Experimental, which was one of the main hubs of Chilean film culture throughout the 1960s and early 1970s.[57] For this reason, the cinematheque was dismantled by the military soon after the coup. In 2004, after a series of internal negotiations, two university departments agreed on a protocol of collaboration and shared funding that eventually led to the reopening of the cinematheque in 2008, under the direction of legendary filmmaker

Figure 2. Documentation housed in the Archivo Ruiz-Sarmiento, Instituto de Arte de la Pontificia Universidad Católica de Valparaíso.

Pedro Chaskel, who had also headed the institution in the early 1960s.[58] The immense temporal gap between Cineteca de la Universidad de Chile's official closure in 1976 and its reopening in 2008 evidences the financial and political difficulties in the rebuilding of the cultural apparatus of the state after the regaining of democracy in 1990. But this thirty-year interval should not be taken as a sign that there were no archival efforts before the early 2000s. An unavoidable institution in this regard is Cinemateca Chilena de la Resistencia, later called Cinemateca Chilena en el Exilio (in what follows, I will refer to it simply as Cinemateca Chilena to avoid confusion arising from its dual name). Although a history of this organization exceeds the scope of this article, a few important traits must be sketched. Cinemateca Chilena was founded in exile in 1974 by filmmakers Pedro Chaskel and Gastón Ancelovici and was conceived as the "logical continuation" of Cineteca de la Universidad de Chile and the future center for collecting Chilean cinema in exile.[59] Cinemateca Chilena is hard to classify under traditional labels, because it adopts different forms (a film archive, a center for documentation and research, a production and distribution company, a not-for-profit foundation) and operates simultaneously in several countries (Cuba, France, Spain, Canada). Sharing multiple locations while lacking any fixed position, Cinemateca Chilena is an exilic institution by definition.

Its importance resides in the fact that it became an effort to articulate Chilean exile cinema despite its scattered nature. Cinemateca Chilena kept prints in film archives in Cuba and Spain. The organization's structure—and especially its status as an extension of the dismantled University of Chile's Cinematheque—allowed Cinemateca Chilena to relate institutionally with film festivals, production companies, film archives, and FIAF.[60] Even if participation in FIAF congresses was marginal, Cinemateca Chilena's presence evidences the need to be visible in global archival networks together with the desire to act as an official representative of the "Chilean" archival institutions, but in and from the interstitial spaces of exile.[61] In this sense, Cinemateca Chilena must be read as a bridge— an attempt to establish an institutional continuity despite the radical rupture marked by the coup. Chaskel's figure is fundamentally strategic here, as he himself embodies this institutional bridge: first as director of Cineteca de la Universidad de Chile before the coup, then as head of Cinemateca Chilena together with Gastón Ancelovici, and later once again as director of the university's cinematheque when it reopened in Chile in 2008.[62]

Since its reopening, Cineteca de la Universidad de Chile has managed to secure donations from exile filmmakers, especially those associated with Cine Experimental, like Chaskel. The state university cinematheque has also digitized a series of exile films that are part of its virtual platform and has organized, curated, and sponsored various film programs related to Chilean exile cinema.[63] In addition, Cineteca is currently digitizing the Fondo Zuzana Pick, an immense donation made by this pioneer scholar of Chilean exile cinema in 2016 composed of nearly three thousand documents (correspondence, manuscripts, press clippings, handwritten notes, photographs, posters, etc.).[64]

The following institution presents a fundamental difference from the other three in the group, because it is a museum with a pedagogical and ethical mandate at the same time as it constitutes a "site of memory," one of those social spaces for the circulation of memories and elaboration of traumatic experiences, as Elizabeth Jelin defined them in relation to the postdictatorships of the Southern Cone.[65] In the context of the Bicentennial of the Republic of Chile, Museo de la Memoria y los Derechos Humanos (Museum of Memory and Human Rights) was created in 2010 with the mission of giving visibility to human rights violations committed by the state of Chile between 1973 and 1990 so as to ensure that "actions that affect the dignity of human beings are never again repeated."[66] Its Audiovisual Archive has existed since the creation of the museum and operates under the same mission.[67] Museo de la Memoria receives an annual direct subsidy from the state, regulated by the National Budget. This funding has come under scrutiny almost every year, which points to a still unachieved social and political consensus regarding the country's recent past and the museum's role in it. Frequent criticisms that center on the institution's strict temporal demarcation, its definition of who is a victim of human rights abuses (based on the official 1991 Rettig Report), and its fundamental conception as a project of "moral reparation" all suggest that it is the museum's very existence that is questioned.[68] Public suspicion of the museum, especially coming from the right-wing sectors of society that supported the dictatorship, evidences a fraught context of memory debates. The presence of Chilean exile titles in the collections of the Museum of Memory must therefore be understood within this broader landscape of memory as "battleground."[69]

Throughout the years, the museum has given space to the specific remembrances of exile in exhibits, websites, oral history projects, and video testimonies. This interest had its peak in 2014, when the entire programming was devoted to the topic of "exile and asylum," including two important film series.[70] In terms of collection development, the legal mandate of the museum forbids the acquisition of documents, films, or artworks; it can only receive donations from individuals or institutions. For this reason, its audiovisual archive, composed of approximately twenty-four hundred titles, has been mostly created out of filmmakers' personal donations. Rare exile titles like *Re-torno* (David Benavente, Netherlands/Chile, 1983) and *Conversación en el exilio con Raúl Ampuero* (Rafael Guzmán, Italy, 1986) are part of the museum's audiovisual collection.[71] Securing donations from international institutions, particularly European TV networks like the BBC, RAI, or ZDF and national agencies like France's INA, which have provided plenty of interviews, newsreels, and television documentaries related to Chilean exiles, has also been a goal of the museum.

The museum's interest in films and other audiovisual works about exile exceeds Chilean exile cinema, if we understand the latter as those films made by Chilean exile directors throughout the world, thus pointing toward a much vaster media universe of the Chilean exile experience. In this museum, Chilean exile cinema dissolves into all kinds of audiovisual pieces that are only thematically connected to exile. Both in the development of its archival collection and in its public programming, the approach privileges the presence of contemporary documentaries that deal with the psychological and cultural aftermaths of exile. The museum's lens for safeguarding and presenting exile cinema is subjected to an ethical understanding of exile as a violation of human rights. Above all, it presents all exile films, whether fictional or not, exclusively as *documents* and evidentiary proof of the exile experience. This experiential approach has nonetheless an important political advantage, as it favors the activation of social memories of exile that are geared toward the future. This is particularly evident in the museum's exhibition practice, which always involves some form of public discussion where different

Figure 3. The three vaults of Cineteca Nacional de Chile in Santiago safeguard more than five thousand titles. Courtesy of Cineteca Nacional de Chile.

generations of exiles and other victims of the dictatorship meet. Filmic returns are in this sense "embodied" in a collective reelaboration of memory.

Cineteca Nacional de Chile was created in 2006 and immediately became the foremost film archive in the country (Figure 3). As Chile's National Film Archive, Cineteca Nacional has been a FIAF member since 2009. In terms of its legal constitution, as in many other cases of the Chilean cultural scene, its status functions under a semifictitious notion of "public." While theoretically a state institution, Cineteca Nacional depends on the Centro Cultural Palacio la Moneda, a private nonprofit foundation from which it receives a basic operational budget. Law 21.045, which created the Ministry of Cultures, the Arts, and Patrimony in 2018, includes Cineteca Nacional as one of the institutions that would become part of the National Service of Cultural Heritage and would therefore receive direct funding from the state. However, an official transfer has yet to occur.[72] Until that happens, Cineteca Nacional is forced to apply to different public funding instruments, competing with other local archives and museums to fund its different preservation, exhibition, and educational programs.

Given this lack of resources, Chilean exile cinema has never been a priority for Cineteca Nacional, as the repatriation and restoration projects of early newsreels, the few extant silent features, and films produced by the national studio Chile Films in the 1940s have been deemed more urgent. The corpus of Chilean exile cinema has entered the collections of Cineteca Nacional mostly thanks to donations from individual filmmakers, through a deposit agreement that regulates the safeguarding of the material and determines rights for public exhibition. At least fourteen Chilean exile filmmakers have donated DVDs, Betacam tapes, 16mm and 35mm prints, and original negatives and sound elements (if available).[73] Another donation worth mentioning is the one by the Russian studio Mosfilm, which sent 35mm prints of all the features Sebastián Alarcón directed for the studio.[74] Owing to its FIAF membership, Cineteca Nacional has also been able to sign contracts of collaboration, such as the 2009 agreement with ICAIC and Cinemateca de Cuba that enabled the return of 35mm prints of Littin's *El recurso del método* (Mexico/Cuba/France, 1978) and *Alsino y el Cóndor* (Nicaragua/Cuba/Mexico/Costa Rica, 1982). More recently, organizing film series has meant new protocols of cooperation, such as the one signed with Cinémathèque française and INA to program, in August 2016, *¡Celebremos a Ruiz!,* a smaller iteration of the seventy-film series that Cinémathèque française had presented a few months earlier in Paris.[75]

ARCHIVAL ONLINE PLATFORMS AND DIGITAL RETURNS

Most film archives currently have a website or digital platform where titles from their collections are highlighted. These films can be seen in their entirety and usually, though not always, without geographic restriction. The rise of online viewing sites run by archives is a consequence of a mixture of factors, including (1) the current emphasis on digitization projects, especially prevalent in archives with strong and steady public funding; (2) the need to open up to new publics and to understand digital access as a "core responsibility"; and (3) the industry turn toward streaming sites, especially accentuated after the Covid-19 pandemic in 2020.[76] Online viewability of what used to be rare archival materials, available only to a limited number of scholars, programmers, and archivists, constitutes a recent phenomenon that indicates a shift in archival practice compared to the situation ten years ago. In the case of Chilean exile films, the change is significant. To be able to watch a Chilean exile film, one had to get it directly from the filmmaker (who often did not have it), or one had to travel. In January 2014, I made a trip to different archives in Montreal, Ottawa, and Toronto—the only way to be able to watch the many films Chilean exiles had made in Canada. Years later, in 2017, the aforementioned *Il n'y a pas d'oubli*, arguably one of the most important Chilean exile titles together with *Diálogos de exiliados* (Raúl Ruiz, France, 1974), was digitized and uploaded to the website of the National Film Board of Canada (NFB), the organization that produced the film in 1975. Besides simply typing out its title, users of the NFB platform will encounter this film through keywords such as "political refugees," "integration of immigrants in Quebec," and "lifestyle of immigrants." Other Chilean exile films currently available on the NFB website include the Challenge for Change production *Les Borges* (Marilú Mallet, 1978) and more recent films like *Chile, Obstinate Memory* (Patricio Guzmán, 1997).[77]

Throughout the years that I was conducting initial research on the history of Chilean exile cinema, one film was particularly elusive—*Lettre du Chili* (Marcos Galo, France, 1978). I could not locate a copy, and there was no information on the film except for its title, director, year, and place of production—data that were part of Pick's 1984 exile filmography. In 2018, watching the archive footage documentary *The Trial* (Sergei Loznitsa, 2018), I became aware of the existence of the French Communist Party's film archive Ciné-Archives. Out of mere curiosity, I browsed the website, and there it was, available online for everyone to view. Ciné-Archives safeguards the works made by the film production cooperative of the party, Unicité.[78] For this reason, it currently holds two 16mm prints of *Lettre du Chili* in its Bobigny vaults. According to archivist Marion Boulestreau, the film was a Unicité project developed by a French team. There are no certainties about Chilean exile Marcos Galo's role as director. It is not clear, either, why the name "Unicité" was removed from the credits.[79] Despite the historical uncertainties regarding this film, it is an extraordinary finding that deserves more visibility. The images are composed exclusively of *arpilleras* (sackcloth) made by working-class women during the dictatorship. Spoken in French, the film is structured as a letter sent by one of those women from Chile out to the world.

Other digital platforms created by international archives that currently hold Chilean exile titles include SFI's Filmarkivet.se, where the exile short film *Clownens dröm* (Luis Vera, 1981) can be seen, and Cinémathèque française's Henri, which uploaded five titles by Raúl Ruiz shortly after the launch of the streaming platform in April 2020.[80] These initiatives guarantee greater access to Chilean exile cinema, both by a national audience in Chile and by diasporic communities abroad; however, not all difficulties are resolved. The linguistic challenge remains, because none of the international archives that I have mentioned offers Spanish subtitles or captions, and the curatorial gaze upon the films in question is dependent on the historical narrative proposed by the foreign archive (as seen by the keywords used by NFB). Most importantly, Chilean exile films that are part of the online platforms of international archives are still a minority. Most remain safeguarded exclusively in 16mm or 35mm prints.

Chilean film archives have also been part of the boom of digital platforms.[81] Launched in 2011, the first one was Cineteca de la Universidad de Chile's Cineteca Virtual, which uses a Creative Commons license and has a specific category dedicated to Chilean exile cinema that includes digital files of films like Pedro Chaskel's *Los ojos como mi papá* (1979) and various other titles he directed for Cuba's ICAIC; Rodrigo Gonçalves's works for the Instituto Nacional do Cinema in Maputo, Mozambique; and the important historical documentary *Los puños frente al cañón* (Orlando Lübbert and Gastón Ancelovici, West Germany, 1975).[82] Privileging access over resolution, these online versions constitute an example of what Tadeo Fuica and Keldjian have termed "palimpsestic digital copies," where "different layers of material conversion" can be seen.[83] While data associated with each title often contain dates, place of production, cast and crew, and a synopsis, specific historical and archival information about original materials, restoration, and digitization processes is either absent or vague. Like Cineteca Virtual, Cineteca Nacional de Chile's Cineteca Nacional Online followed in 2013 under the vision that there is no preservation if it does not go hand in hand with access.[84] The platform is part of the national film archive's broader digitization initiative that has allowed them to digitize 731 16mm and 35mm titles and more than 1,500 Super 8mm home movies on its 2K and 4K scanners, which are then stored as LTO7 tapes and DPX files.[85] Films made in exile by directors like Orlando Lübbert, Miguel Littin, and Leo Mendoza, among many others, can be found here. More recently, Museo de la Memoria y los Derechos Humanos created Conectados con la Memoria, a digital platform with a streaming component where some Chilean exile films and other titles related to the experience of exile can be viewed.[86]

These three archives emphasize how digital platforms enable a greater access to filmic heritage, especially in an excessively centralized country like Chile, where most cultural institutions function in the capital, Santiago. There are even more utopic visions, such as the one espoused by Luis Horta, head of Cineteca de la Universidad de Chile. Horta conceives the digital space as an opportunity to "re-signify the political use of the archive through education and outreach," in the understanding that the archive exists as such only once it is "appropriated by audiences."[87] What is missing in many of these comments is a more critical view of the neoliberal rhetoric of immediate "access" to "contents"—terms that are all loaded with ideology and that efface the material con-stitution of films as artifacts.[88] The three Chilean websites that I have discussed could benefit more from the possibilities offered by a digital environment that enables new forms of appearances of exile films, as Ignacio Albornoz Fariña has suggested in relation to the online platforms of university archives in Chile.[89] This reflection is especially needed with regard to the handling and presentation of archival metadata that could offer new insights into the material history of exile films and their multilingualism and plurality of geographical displacements. Last, the content presented in Conectados con la Memoria and Cineteca Virtual tends to be deprived of a curatorial and historical narrative. Curatorship is key, because its interpretative task is what "differentiates a collecting body from a mere repository of audiovisual content."[90] Cineteca Nacional Online, in turn, favors interpretation through what it calls "online specials," thematic or historical groupings that are presented with a brief introductory text. In light of this research project, I collaborated with Cineteca Nacional, coprogramming a selection of ten Chilean exile films that were already part of the website's contents but that usually go unnoticed by viewers and users of the site. The special was introduced by a clear and simple narrative detailing some of the main cinematic, historical, and political dimensions of Chilean exile cinema.[91] Curatorship for this program evidences the geographic diversity of the corpus and puts in dialogue short-, medium-, and feature-length fictions, documentaries, and experimental projects.

In this article, I have historicized the archival returns of exile cinema to Chilean archives and museums, while also discussing the presence of this diasporic corpus in several international institutions. The cinematheques, museums, and film archives that have interested me here are the material spaces where technical and curatorial protocols are negotiated with particular institutional and administrative settings and with specific cultural expectations. Film archives are no mere repositories but fundamental "historical actors" that participate in wider social and cultural processes.[92] With this in mind, I have demonstrated that the incomplete and unfinished phenomenon of archival return is due in great part to the difficulties that the exile corpus involves, as well as to the specific nature and financial/political limitations of the four Chilean institutions analyzed in this study. Archival returns to Chile have not responded to an official policy by the cultural apparatus of the Chilean state, nor have they been the result of a set of sustained curatorial guidelines of archives and museums addressing Chilean exile cinema as a whole. Rather, archival returns have taken place thanks to partial efforts related to projects involving particular films and the careers of a reduced number of filmmakers. Archivo Ruiz-Sarmiento favors an auteurist lens restricted to only two directorial figures. Cineteca de la Universidad de Chile espouses a vision of Chilean exile cinema that emphasizes the role of those individuals historically associated with the university

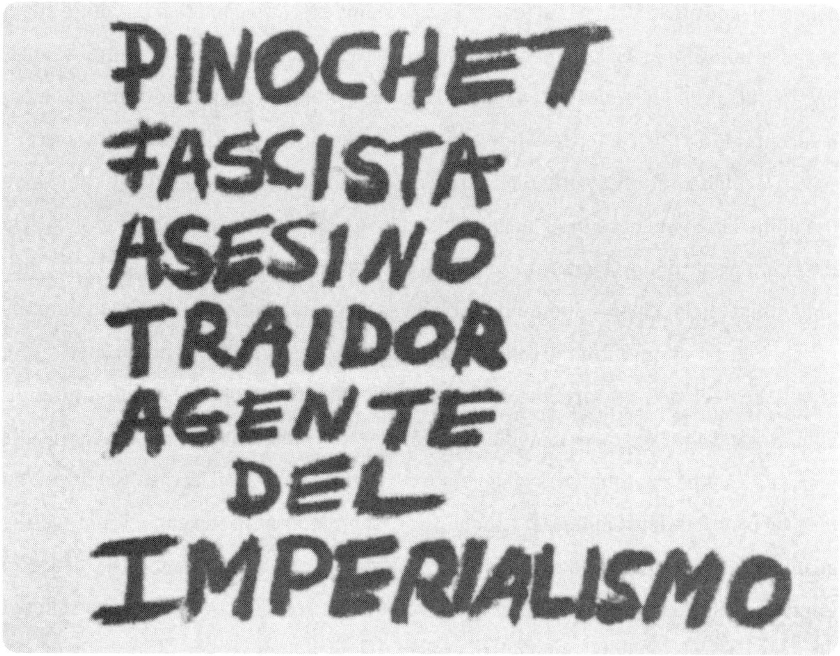

PINOCHET
FASCISTA
ASESINO
TRAIDOR
AGENTE
DEL
IMPERIALISMO

Figure 4. Screen grab from *Pinochet: fascista, asesino, traidor, agente del imperialismo* (Sergio Castilla, 1974), one of the seven titles recently digitized and returned to Chile thanks to an agreement between Cineteca Nacional de Chile and the Swedish Film Institute. Courtesy of Cineteca Nacional de Chile.

cinematheque in the late 1960s and early 1970s. Museo de la Memoria y los Derechos Humanos concentrates on the evidentiary power of Chilean exile films (*documents* of the experience of exile understood as a human rights violation) and on its ability to activate memories and transgenerational dialogue about the lasting effects of displacement. Cineteca Nacional de Chile favors the return of exile films whose themes or approach are explicitly "Chilean," thus proving how challenging exile continues to be for an institutional film history still anchored within the geographical and ideological boundaries of the nation and its heritage.

The notion of archival returns stresses the various challenges that the transnationality, mobility, and inherent in-betweenness of exile cinemas pose for the institution of the archive. Archives and museums remain deeply rooted in the national as their main operative framework, even if they are not "national" archives properly speaking, and even if they engage in international exchanges via global networks like FIAF. As I previously suggested, the idea of an archival return does not do away with these challenges, as it will always presuppose, if not a homeland, at least a site of origin (even if this origin does not coincide with its actual place of production). In this regard, archival websites and streaming platforms enable what might be called "digital returns"—spaces of virtual collection and presentation that are not tied to a single location and that therefore might be more suited for an exile cinema with various national affiliations and cultural belongings.[93] The *digital* in *digital return* should also indicate, as Caroline Frick has claimed, a decentered archival practice where more diverse actors and publics can participate.[94]

Digital returns, furthermore, rely on cost-effective practices that better serve the limited budgets of Latin American film archives, as they do not necessarily involve the shipping of 16mm or 35mm prints. In light of the research project that led to the writing of this article, I also elaborated for Cineteca Nacional de Chile a short filmography of exile titles that are currently safeguarded in international archives and whose return should be deemed a priority. We are now initiating a process of collaboration with foreign archives that will favor a model of digital return where both the labor and results of the process of 2K scanning, syncing, and mastering are shared by the provider of the original materials and Cineteca Nacional. The first project, currently under way, involves a collaboration with SFI that will result in the "digital return" of seven titles made by Chileans in Sweden (Figure 4). Future archival research on Chilean exile cinema should also move toward a digital humanities project that could operate under a participatory and postcustodial model of archiving.[95] The digital model of postcustody deemphasizes the physical deposit and in turn stresses decentered administration of a given collection, something especially valuable for an exile filmic corpus that is not attached to any single nation, territory, language, or culture.

José Miguel Palacios is an assistant professor in the Department of Film and Electronic Arts at California State University, Long Beach. His work has appeared in journals such as *Screen, Jump Cut, [in]Transition,* and *Archivos de la Filmoteca,* as well as in various edited collections published in the United States, Argentina, and Chile. He received his PhD from New York University's Department of Cinema Studies in 2017.

NOTES

1. This research was supported by Chile's National Fund for Scientific and Technological Development (FONDECYT) through its postdoctoral grant 3180208, "Imagen, archivo, memoria: los retornos del cine chileno del exilio."

2. Nataša Ďurovičová, preface to *World Cinemas, Transnational Perspectives*, ed. Nataša Ďurovičová and Kathleen Newman (New York: Routledge, 2010), x.

3. Asli Özgen and Elif Rongen-Kaynakçi, "The Transnational Archive as a Site of Disruption, Discrepancy, and Decomposition: The Complexities of Ottoman Film Heritage," *The Moving Image* 21, no. 1–2 (2021): 77–99; Giovanna Fossati, "For a Global Approach to Audiovisual Heritage: A Plea for North/South Exchange in Research and Practice," *NECSUS_European Journal of Media Studies* 10, no. 2 (2021): 127–33.

4. Thomas C. Wright and Rody Oñate, "Chilean Political Exile," *Latin American Perspectives* 34, no. 4 (2007): 31.

5. For overviews of Chilean exile cinema, see Zuzana M. Pick, "Chilean Cinema: Ten Years of Exile (1973–1983)," *Jump Cut*, no. 32 (1987), http://www.ejumpcut.org/archive/onlinessays/JC32folder/ChileanFilmExile.html, and Jacqueline Mouesca, *Plano secuencia de la memoria de chile: veinticinco años de cine chileno (1960–1985)* (Madrid: Ediciones del Litoral, 1988), 137–58.

6. Pick, "Chilean Cinema."

7. For particular examples of the variety of modes of production found by Chilean filmmakers in exile, see José Miguel Palacios, "Resistance vs. Exile: The Political Rhetoric of Chilean Exile Cinema in the 1970s," *Jump Cut*, no. 57 (2016), https://ejumpcut.org/archive/jc57.2016/-PalaciosChile/index.html. For a wider understanding of the notion of mode of production in exilic and diasporic cinemas in general, see Hamid Naficy, *An Accented Cinema: Exilic and Diasporic Filmmaking* (Princeton, N.J.: Princeton University Press, 2001), 40–62.

8. María Teresa Johansson and Constanza Vergara, "Filman los hijos: nuevo testimonio en los documentales *En algún lugar del cielo* de Alejandra Carmona y *Mi vida con Carlos* de Germán Berger-Hertz," *Meridional. Revista Chilena de Estudios Latinoamericanos*, no. 2 (April 2014): 89–105; Elizabeth Ramírez-Soto, "Traveling Memories: Women's Reminiscences of Displaced Childhood in Chilean Postdictatorship Documentary," in *Doing Women's Film History: Reframing Cinemas, Past and Future*, ed. Christine Gledhill and Julia Knight, 139–50 (Urbana: University of Illinois Press, 2015).

9. Vázquez's actual words were "Yo me desexilié en 1993" (I de-exiled in 1993). For the term *desexilio*, see Elizabeth Ramírez-Soto, "Journeys of *Desexilio*: The Bridge between the Past and the Present," *Rethinking History* 3, no. 18 (2014): 439, and Mario Benedetti, *El desexilio y otras conjeturas* (Madrid: El País, 1984), 39–42.

10. "It is possible to go into exile voluntarily and then return, yet still not fully arrive" is Naficy's sentence. See Hamid Naficy, "Introduction: Framing

Exile—From Homeland to Homepage," in *Home, Exile, Homeland: Film, Media, and the Politics of Place,* ed. Hamid Naficy (New York: Routledge, 1999), 3.

11. Foundational studies of Chilean exile cinema were developed "in exile" throughout the 1970s and 1980s, fundamentally by scholar Zuzana Pick (originally from Colombia but based in Canada), by Chilean film historian Jacqueline Mouesca (based in France), and by Chilean exile filmmakers Gastón Ancelovici and Pedro Chaskel. In the last decade, together with the creation of archives and the emergence of a new generation of local scholars in Chile, there has been a renewed academic interest in specific directors, topics, and titles of Chilean exile cinema.

12. Elizabeth Ramírez-Soto, "*Habanera*: de fragmentos y retornos inacabados," in *Una mirada oblicua: el cine de Valeria Sarmiento,* ed. Bruno Cuneo and Fernando Pérez V., 89–101 (Santiago: Universidad Alberto Hurtado, 2021).

13. Janet Ceja Alcalá, "Imperfect Archives and the Principle of Social Praxis in the History of Film Preservation in Latin America," *The Moving Image* 13, no. 1 (2013): 81.

14. Hamid Naficy, *The Making of Exile Cultures: Iranian Television in Los Angeles* (Minneapolis: University of Minnesota Press, 1993), 7–10.

15. Laura Marks, *The Skin of the Film: Intercultural Cinema, Embodiment, and the Senses* (Durham, N.C.: Duke University Press, 2000); Ella Shohat and Robert Stam, eds., *Multiculturalism, Postcoloniality, and Transnational Media* (New Brunswick, N.J.: Rutgers University Press, 2003); Elizabeth Ezra and Terry Rowden, eds., *Transnational Cinema: The Film Reader* (New York: Routledge, 2006); Naficy, *An Accented Cinema.*

16. For a more detailed explanation, see José Miguel Palacios, "Chilean Exile Cinema and Its Homecoming Documentaries," in *Cinematic Homecomings: Exile and Return in Transnational Cinemas,* ed. Rebecca Prime (New York: Bloomsbury, 2015), 151–52.

17. Caroline Frick, *Saving Cinema: The Politics of Preservation* (Oxford: Oxford University Press, 2011), 13.

18. Adelheid Heftberger, "The Current Landscape of Film Archiving and How Study Programs Can Contribute," *Synoptique: An Online Journal of Film and Moving Image Studies* 6, no. 1 (2018): 58.

19. Derek Gillman, *The Idea of Cultural Heritage,* rev. ed. (Cambridge: Cambridge University Press, 2010), 44–49; Frick, *Saving Cinema,* 14, 159.

20. Paolo Cherchi Usai, "The Politics of Film Repatriation" (paper presented at the Seventh Orphan Film Symposium, New York, April 2010).

21. Caroline Frick, "Repatriating American Film Heritage or Heritage Hoarding?," *Convergence: The International Journal of Research into New Media Technologies* 21, no. 1 (2014): 3.

22. Andrew Prescott, "Archives of Exile, Exile of Archives," in *What Are Archives? Cultural and Theoretical Perspectives: A Reader,* ed. Louise Craven (Aldershot, U.K.: 2008), 133.

23. Cherchi Usai, "Politics of Film Repatriation."

24. Cherchi Usai.

25. Kirsten Weld, *Paper Cadavers: The Archives of Dictatorship in Guatemala* (Durham, N.C.: Duke University Press, 2014), 13.

26. Paulo Antonio Paranaguá and Gastón Ancelovici, "Cine chileno del exilio," *Araucaria de Chile,* no. 14 (1981): 197; Zuzana M. Pick, "Tradición y búsqueda (1973–1983)," *Araucaria de Chile,* no. 23 (1985): 103; Pick, "Chilean Cinema."

27. Zuzana M. Pick, "Cronología del cine chileno en el exilio 1973/1983," *Literatura Chilena: Creación y Crítica,* no. 27 (Winter 1984): 15–21.

28. Cineteca Nacional de Chile, *Imágenes de Chile en el mundo: Catastro del acervo audiovisual chileno en el exterior* (Santiago, Chile: Cineteca Nacional de Chile, 2008), 8.

29. Cineteca Nacional de Chile, 8–9.

30. Archives with open catalogs that were researched for this project include Eye Filmmuseum (Eye), British Film Institute, Arsenal–Institut für Film und Videokunst (Arsenal), Deutsche Kinemathek, Berkeley Art Museum and Pacific Film Archive, and Fondazione Archivio Audiovisivo del Movimento Operaio e Democratico. About some archives' recent "bold" step to make their catalogs and data openly available online, see Heftberger, "Current Landscape of Film Archiving," 61.

31. A provisional list of lost or yet to be found Chilean exile films includes *Patria dulce* (Beatriz González, 1976), *Margarita Naranjo* (Álvaro Ramírez, 1976), *La noche del capitán* (Luis Mora, 1977), *Siempre seremos ucranianos* (Leutén Rojas, 1977), *Lota '73* (Álvaro Ramírez, 1977), *Casamiento de negros* (José Echevarría, 1978), *La batalla contra el miedo* (Marcos Galo, 1979), *La escuela* (Reinaldo Zambrano, 1980), *El tren en la ventana* (Leonardo de la Barra, 1981), and *Chez Mascotte* (Leonardo de la Barra, 1981).

32. Beatriz Tadeo Fuica and Julieta Keldjian, "Digital Super 8mm: Evaluating the Contribution of Digital Technologies to Film Archives in Latin America," *The Moving Image* 16, no. 2 (2016): 78.

33. Ramírez-Soto, "*Habanera.*"

34. While the central focus of this article is placed on institutional archives, it is important to remember that these are not the sole places holding rare exilic materials. Informal archives and personal collections of directors, producers, and their heirs are crucial sites to hunt for Chilean exile films.

35. Dan Streible, "The State of Orphan Films: Editor's Introduction," *The Moving Image* 9, no. 1 (2009): x.

36. Streible, x.

37. Raúl Ruiz Film and Videotape Collection, 1960–1996, David M. Rubenstein Rare Book Manuscript Library, Duke University Libraries, https://archives.lib.duke.edu/catalog/ruizraul.

38. A similar task is currently taking place with filmic elements from another unfinished Ruiz film stored in the Duke collection, *El realismo socialista considerado como una de las bellas artes,* shot in 1973 with an original expected completion date of 2023. See Rodrigo González, "La Unidad Popular según Raúl Ruiz," *La Tercera,* May 9, 2020, https://www.latercera.com/culto/2020/05/09/la-unidad-popular-segun-raul-ruiz/.

39. I thank Floris Paalman for generously sharing a provisional list of Chilean prints in the collections of the International Institute of Social History. Paalman, email correspondence with the author, August 25, 2019.

40. For a history of this Dutch cine-club, see Luna Hupperetz, "Militant

Film Circuit of Cineclub Vrijheidsfilms," Orphan Film Symposium, May 9, 2020, https://wp.nyu.edu/orphanfilm/2020/05/29/vrijheidsfilms/. Please also see Luna Hupperetz, "Cineclub Vrijheidsfilms: Restoring a Militant Cinema Network," *The Moving Image* 22, no. 1 (2022): 46–64.

41. For a detailed account of the relationship between Arsenal and Chilean cinema, see Mónica Villarroel and Isabel Mardones, *Señales contra el olvido: cine chileno recobrado* (Santiago: Cuarto Propio, 2012), 48–65, 85–117, 149–59. See also "Film Database," Arsenal–Institut für Film und Videokunst, http://films.arsenal-berlin.de/.

42. Swedish Film Database, http://www.svenskfilmdatabas.se/en/.

43. Jon Wengström, Senior Curator, SFI, email correspondence with the author, June 11, 2020.

44. Fondos Fílmicos, Filmoteca Española, email correspondence with the author, December 3 and 4, 2018.

45. For a short history of other Chilean film archives, see Mónica Villarroel, "Cineteca Nacional de Chile: dilemas y desafíos en tiempos digitales," *Imagofagia*, no. 22 (2020): 390–91.

46. Though not an archive, properly speaking, another actor worth mentioning in this process of return is Goethe-Institut Santiago. Through the work of its cinematheque director Isabel Mardones, Goethe-Institut has been instrumental in bringing digital files of exile films by Antonio Skármeta, Carlos Puccio, Juan Forch, and Vivienne Barry and has been a frequent collaborator with Cineteca Nacional de Chile, Cineteca de la Universidad de Chile, and Museo de la Memoria in their public programs.

47. Manuel Martínez Carril, "Half a Century of Film Archives in Latin America," *Bulletin FIAF*, no. 44 (1992): 5.

48. Maria Rita Galvão, "La situación del patrimonio fílmico en Iberoamérica," *Journal of Film Preservation*, no. 71 (2006): 44.

49. Rielle Navitski, "Reconsidering the Archive: Digitization and Latin American Film Historiography," *Cinema Journal* 54, no. 1 (2014): 121. See also Juana Suárez, "New Buildings, New Pathways: Toward Dynamic Archives in Latin America and the Caribbean," *The Moving Image* 21, no. 1–2 (2021): 26–54.

50. See Bruno Cuneo's and Luis Horta's interventions in the online dialogue "Fondos documentales e investigación sobre cine chileno del exilio," Universidad Alberto Hurtado, November 17, 2020, https://www.youtube.com/watch?v=XNO0SNqBzWk. See also Frick, *Saving Cinema*, 114–15, 153, and Rielle Navitski, "Toward a Global Film Preservation Movement? Institutional Histories of Film Archiving in Latin America," *Journal of Cinema and Media Studies* 60, no. 4 (2021): 188–90.

51. A video presentation can be found in Archivo Ruiz-Sarmiento, Pontificia Universidad Católica de Valparaíso, https://www.youtube.com/watch?v=sWG5kq2lhdc.

52. Elizabeth Ramírez-Soto, "The Double Day of Valeria Sarmiento: Exile, Precariousness, and Cinema's Gendered Division of Labor," *Feminist Media Histories* 7, no. 3 (2021): 154–77.

53. Archivo Ruiz-Sarmiento, Instituto de Arte PUCV, Catálogo Patrimonio Documental, 2014–19. I thank Bruno Cuneo for generously sharing this unpublished document with me.

54. Cuneo and Horta, "Fondos documentales."

55. Cuneo and Horta.

56. "Ruiz, Raoul (1941–2011)," La collection de l'IMEC, https://www.imec -archives.com/archives/collection/AU/FR_145875401_P487RUZ. These ma-terials were also donated by Sarmiento.

57. Claudio Salinas Muñoz and Hans Stange, *Historia del cine experimental en la Universidad de Chile 1957–1973* (Santiago: Uqbar, 2008).

58. "Historia," Cineteca, Universidad de Chile, https://www.uchile.cl/portal /extension-y-cultura/cineteca/presentacion/58993/historia, and "Historia," Cineteca Virtual, Universidad de Chile, http://cinetecavirtual.uchile.cl/cine teca/index.php/About/Index. See also Salinas Muñoz and Stange, *Historia del Cine Experimental*, 87–90.

59. Pedro Chaskel, "Informe de la secretaría general de UCAL al VII congreso. Caracas, 1974," in *Por un cine latinoamericano: encuentro de cineastas lati-noamericanos en solidaridad con el pueblo y los cineastas de Chile. Caracas, Septiembre de 1974* (Caracas: Rocinante, 1974), 67–68.

60. Gastón Ancelovici to Manfred Lichtenstein, May 2, 1983, BArch DR 140-299/DR 140-365, Bundesarchiv. I thank Isabel Mardones for generously sharing this material with me.

61. FIAF, "Rapport du secrétariat général de l'UCAL à l'assemblée générale du XXXI congrès de la FIAF," Annex 8, Appendices (Torino, June 2–5, 1975), 26– 33, https://www.fiafnet.org/images/tinyUpload/E-Resources/Official -Documents/Protected%20Files/Congress-Reports/1975-AppendicesRED.pdf; Appendices, https://www.fiafnet.org/images/tinyUpload/E-Resources/Official -Documents/Protected%20Files/Congress-Reports/1975-AppendicesRED.pdf; FIAF, Minutes of the Congress and General Meeting (Mexico City, May 24– 27, 1976), https://www.fiafnet.org/images/tinyUpload/E-Resources/Official -Documents/Protected%20Files/Congress-Reports/1976-Mexico%20GA%20 MinutesRED.pdf.

62. In addition to representing an institutional bridge throughout the history of film archives in Chile, Chaskel's own biography—as someone who escaped with his family from the Nazis in Germany and arrived in Chile as a child, only to be forced into a new exile in Cuba after the 1973 military coup—also embodies a broader history of twentieth-century displacements.

63. Among others, "Ciclo de cine chileno del exilio en Casa Central," Uni-versidad de Chile, http://www.uchile.cl/noticias/126050/ciclo-de-cine -chileno-del-exilio-en-casa-central.

64. Cineteca Universidad de Chile, "Centro de documentación," http://col lectiveaccess.cinetecavirtual.uchile.cl/cineteca/index.php/About/centro-de-documentacion.

65. Elizabeth Jelin, *State Repression and the Labors of Memory* (Minneapo-lis: University of Minnesota Press, 2003), 44. See also Pierre Nora, "Between Memory and History: Les Lieux de Mémoire," trans. Marc Roudebush, *Repre-sentations*, no. 26 (1989): 7–24.

66. Museo de la Memoria y los Derechos Humanos, "Definiciones estratégi-cas," https://web.museodelamemoria.cl/sobre-el-museo/definiciones-estrate gicas/.

67. For a detailed discussion of the Museum of Memory and its audiovisual collection, see Kate Adlena Cronin, "'Communication in Service of the

People': Activating Audiovisual Human Rights Collections in Chile," *The Moving Image* 21, no. 1–2 (2021): 100–117.

68. Mauro Basaure, "Museo de la Memoria en conflicto," *Anuari del conflicte social,* no. 4 (2015): 659–85; Basaure, "Hacia una reconstrucción de los conflictos de la memoria: el caso del Museo de la Memoria y los Derechos Humanos en Chile," *MAD,* no. 37 (2017): 113–42; Minerva Campos Rabadán, "La propuesta audiovisual y el discurso del Museo de la Memoria y los Derechos Humanos de Santiago de Chile," *Fotocinema,* no. 20 (2020): 294; Cronin, "Communication in Service of the People," 108–13.

69. Steve Stern, "Introduction to the Trilogy: The Memory Box of Pinochet's Chile," in *Remembering Pinochet's Chile: On the Eve of London 1998* (Durham, N.C.: Duke University Press, 2004), xx.

70. *Ciclo de cine chileno sobre el exilio* ran from August to December 2014 and included twenty-nine films. In addition, *Desexilio del cine chileno: 40 años de la Cinemateca Chilena del Exilio* was co-organized with Cineteca de la Universidad de Chile as an homage to the work of Chaskel's and Ancelovici's Cinemateca Chilena. This program included eleven films and ran from September to November 2014. See Museo de la Memoria y los Derechos Humanos, "Memoria Anual," 2014, 51, https://web.museodelamemoria.cl /wp-content/files_mf/1460129457MEMORIA2014.pdf.

71. The catalog of the museum's audiovisual archive was published as a book in 2015. See *Archivo Audiovisual: colección del Museo de la Memoria y los Derechos Humanos* (Santiago: Ocho Libros/Museo de la Memoria y los Derechos Humanos, 2015). For more updated information on the museum's film and video holdings, see José Manuel Rodríguez's intervention in the online dialogue "Recuperando el cine chileno del exilio," Universidad Alberto Hurtado, December 12, 2020, https://www.youtube.com/watch?v=92wbm90jxcA.

72. Ley 21.045, *Biblioteca del Congreso Nacional de Chile,* https://www .bcn.cl/leychile/navegar?idNorma=1110097. See also Villarroel, "Cineteca Nacional de Chile," 390–91.

73. I thank Cineteca Nacional's former director, Mónica Villarroel, and its former head of documentation, now director, Marcelo Morales, for facilitating access to these agreements.

74. Villarroel, "Cineteca Nacional de Chile," 394.

75. Cinémathèque française, "Raoul Ruiz: du 30 Mars au 30 Mai 2016," http://www.cinematheque.fr/cycle/raoul-ruiz-315.html; Cineteca Nacional de Chile, *¡Celebremos a Ruiz!,* program, August 2016.

76. Floris Paalman, Giovanna Fossati, and Eef Masson, "Introduction: Activating the Archive," *The Moving Image* 21, no. 1–2 (2021): 2.

77. NFB, *Il n'y a pas d'oubli,* https://www.nfb.ca/film/il_n_y_a_pas_doubli/; *Les Borges,* https://www.nfb.ca/film/borges/; *Chile, Obstinate Memory,* https://www.nfb.ca/film/chili_la_memoire_obstinee/.

78. See Céline Barthonnat, "L'audiovisuel au service du Parti communiste français (1968–1976)," in *Des radios de lutte à Internet: militantismes médiatiques et numériques,* ed. Françoise Blum, 137–51 (Paris: Publications de la Sorbonne, 2012), and "Coopérative de production et de diffusion du film (CPDF) et SARL Unité cinéma télévision (Unicité), 1945–1994," 206J/1-345, Archives départementales de la Seine-Saint-Denis, https://docplayer

.fr/55344493-Cooperative-de-production-et-de-diffusion-du-film-cpdf-et-sarl
-unite-cinema-television-unicite.html.

79. Marion Boulestreau, email correspondence with the author, December 6, 2018.

80. See Filmarkivet.se, *Clownens dröm*, https://www.filmarkivet.se/movies
/clownens-drom/. For SFI's digitization practices, see Frida Bonatti and Per Legelius, "How I Learned to Stop Worrying and Love Digital Archives: Digital Archiving Practices at the Swedish Film Institute," *The Moving Image* 19, no. 1 (2019): 144–50. For Cinémathèque française's Henri, see Henri, "Raoul Ruiz," https://www.cinematheque.fr/henri/#raoul-ruiz.

81. For the broader Latin American scene, see Navitski, "Reconsidering the Archive," 121–28. For studies about the online platforms of Chilean archives, see Luis Horta, "Archivos y recursos: los medios digitales en la preservación del patrimonio fílmico chileno," in *La imagen en las sociedades mediáticas latinoamericanas: actas de la IX Bienal Iberoamericana de Comunicación*, 796–803 (Santiago: Instituto de la Comunicación e Imagen, Universidad de Chile, 2013); Mónica Villarroel, "Los desafíos del archivo online: CineChile.cl y Cinetecanacional.cl," *Secuencias*, no. 47 (2018): 131–33; and Villarroel, "Cineteca Nacional de Chile," 387–404.

82. Cineteca Virtual, Cine chileno del exilio, http://collectiveaccess.cinete-cavirtual.uchile.cl/cineteca/index.php/Browse/objects/facet/collection_facet
/id/34/view/images/key/e7ea7a9363bf62768d1a37a4a0c78efa.

83. Tadeo Fuica and Keldjian, "Digital Super 8mm," 74.

84. Villarroel, "Los desafíos del archivo online," 131. See also Cineteca Nacional de Chile, Cineteca Nacional Online, https://www.cclm.cl/cineteca
-nacional-de-chile/.

85. Villarroel, "Cineteca Nacional de Chile," 397.

86. Until the launch of Conectados con la Memoria, the Museum of Memory did not have a streaming option on its website. On-site, nonetheless, the third floor of the museum houses its Centro de Documentación Audiovisual (CEDAV), a space with several touchscreen monitors for in-room consulta-tion. The catalog offers a rich variety of exile titles.

87. Horta, "Archivos y recursos," 797–800.

88. Paolo Cherchi Usai, David Francis, Alexander Horwath, and Michael Loebenstein, eds., *Film Curatorship: Archives, Museums, and the Digital Marketplace* (Vienna: SYNEMA, 2008), 195. See also Anna McCarthy, "The Fetishism of the Content Commodity and Its Secrets" (IKKM Conference: Being With, Weimar, April 18–20, 2013).

89. Ignacio Albornoz Fariña, "Archivos fílmicos en línea: apuntes en torno al acervo universitario chileno," *Contratexto*, no. 34 (2020): 199.

90. Cherchi Usai et al., *Film Curatorship*, 5.

91. José Miguel Palacios, "El cine chileno en el exilio: diez películas en línea," Centro Cultural La Moneda, December 2020, https://www.cclm.cl
/especial/el-cine-chileno-en-el-exilio/.

92. Antoinette Burton, "Introduction: Archive Fever, Archive Stories," in *Archive Stories: Facts, Fiction, and the Writing of History*, ed. Antoinette Burton (Durham, N.C.: Duke University Press, 2005), 7–9.

93. I borrow the idea of digital returns from Caroline Frick's scheme of "digital repatriation." See Frick, "Repatriating American Film Heritage," 2–3.

94. Frick, 3.

95. I thank Janet Ceja Alcalá for responding to a shorter version of this article (in the form of a virtual talk) and for suggesting the possibilities of the post-custodial model. For literature on postcustody archives, see Gerald Ham, "Archival Strategies for the Post-Custodial Era," *American Archivist* 44, no. 3 (1981): 207–16, and Janet Topp Fargion, "Archiving in a Post-Custodial World: An Audiovisual Perspective," Ethnomusicology: Global Field Recordings, 2019, https://www.ethnomusicology.amdigital.co.uk/Explore/Essays /ToppFargion.

PIRACY AND MEDIA ARCHIVAL ACCESS IN THE DIGITAL ERA

MICAH GOTTLIEB

In 2004, a piece by Chris Anderson for *Wired* magazine described the "long tail of media," envisioning a future where once-obscure films and music would be as readily available as mass-market fare. Streaming services like Netflix and iTunes were starting to "embrace the niche," and the concept of a movie or record album going "out of print" would no longer apply. Recommendation algorithms would create a media environment of discovery and abundance. Or, as Anderson put it, "the cultural benefit of all of this is much more diversity, reversing the blanding effects of a century of distribution scarcity and ending the tyranny of the hit."[1] And yet, in December 2020, shortly after HBO Max and Disney+ announced that much or all of their billion-dollar 2021 slate would be debuting simultaneously online and in theaters, a new *Wired* piece argued that the "platinum age of piracy" was about to begin. The author, Abigail De Kosnik, argued that

> many pirates are also good fans, and they will heavily promote the Warner films they like on social media, which will drive up HBO Max subscriptions and increase the cultural value of whichever of the offerings they like best.... By debuting high-profile projects to massive global audiences through both licit and illicit online mechanisms, Disney ensures that an enormous hype machine will immediately promote those projects.[2]

Although the corporate hold on major distribution channels is not a new phenomenon, the Covid-19 pandemic's collapse of the theatrical window across both mainstream and alternative industries—as well as the shuttering of archives and research facilities—has only increased the trend of file sharing. Today, we know that the long tail of media is a fallacy, as hundreds of thousands of movies and records are not available commercially or on streaming services, the largest of which have since doubled down on original programming and largely elided a library of legacy titles.[3] For artists' and independent cinema, works that have traditionally been produced and distributed outside of corporate or commercial structures, the trend of file sharing or bootlegging can be a primary source of exposure, outside of archival film screenings or boutique label home video releases.[4] As a result, for film archives, a new dilemma has set in around the tension between preservation and access. Though archives were not lending physical items during the 2020 pandemic, some made their digital collections available online for a limited time, through partnerships with curators or arts organizations, such as the San Francisco Cinematheque's showcase of Canyon Cinema's digital restorations of Bruce Baillie's work.[5] These high-quality digital copies inevitably end up on file-sharing websites. Increasingly, it would seem that to achieve and sustain relevance in today's landscape, a media artwork must retain the ability to be shared. The smartphone-only streaming service Quibi, which produced original short-form entertainment aimed at millennials and was launched in April 2020, did not allow viewers to take screenshots or post clips of its content online; the service shuttered operations in December and recently announced plans to sell its media library to media electronics manufacturer Roku,[6] after failed attempts to court buyers like Facebook and NBCUniversal.[7]

As a result of this shifting relationship between media consumers and producers, a market of "mass customization as an alternative to mass-market fare," as Anderson puts it, has indeed arrived—but it has largely occurred outside of the market. Websites like Plex, a personal digital media server, and Karagarga, an underground file-sharing website, have created alternative forms of streaming and archival access available to film enthusiasts and have taken on new relevance in a socially distanced nontheatrical landscape, where the latest blockbusters are necessarily viewed in the same space and context as artists' and independent cinema. With these networks in mind, to what extent can archives place their holdings online, whether for research or public exhibition purposes, and invite the risk of unauthorized copies? How, if at all, does this affect the value of these works? This article examines these alternative forms of distribution and archiving in the digital era and how they embody complex issues around piracy and copyright.

A BRIEF HISTORY OF FILM PIRACY AND COPYRIGHT

The act of piracy has been a part of U.S. film history since film's inception. Paul McDonald writes that "acts of unauthorized duplication, circulation, adaptation and presentation . . . played a formative role in the overall making of the film business."[8] The earliest film producers initiated a series of lawsuits around the practice of "duping," which, according to Peter Decherney, entailed "striking a new negative from a competitor's film and then printing and selling it as part of the duper's own catalogue."[9] Making copies of works by domestic and overseas competitors was a common practice and, ultimately, the supply of films "could not keep up with the growing audience demand, and preventing duping was extremely difficult."[10] Some film companies attempted to self-regulate by devising technical procedures to develop proprietary sprocket hole designs, yet the lack of format interoperability "led companies to make dupes that could be displayed using their own technology. Much as copy protection does today, early film copy protection had the opposite of its intended effect: it increased the amount of duping."[11] Eventually, this case of duping went to court, as in the case of *Edison v. Lubin* (1903), which examined the Edison Company's practice of printing films on long strips of photographic paper. The case made it illegal to dupe a film that had been registered as a paper print and thus "granted the same protection to moving images as to other types of photography."[12] But this decision "proved difficult to enforce in the decentralised film business."[13] Duping remained a standard practice "until the formation of the Motion Picture Patents Company (MPPC) in 1908 created a centralised, heavily monitored and repressive network of film manufacturers."[14] The relationship between film and preexisting media was further elaborated in the influential 1911 U.S. Supreme Court case *Kalem Co. v. Harper Brothers,* which dealt with adaptations of theatrical works and ruled that producers could be held liable for unauthorized adaptations. "In the long term, the decision established a legal doctrine that has driven the business of media distribution and consumption from the VCR to file sharing. . . . When new technologies are created, investors (and sometimes courts) have to decide whether the inventors have designed a tool for the sole purpose of facilitating piracy or if they are fostering a new media revolution."[15] The following year, Congressman Edward Townsend pushed an amendment to the Copyright Act of 1909, adding "two categories of subject matter: photoplays of dramatic subject matters; and other forms of moving images based on factual material (i.e. newsreels)"—wherein moving images finally became recognized as a distinct medium under U.S. copyright legislation. As such, the origins of "Hollywood" dovetailed with the accommodation of film into the culture of copyright protection.[16]

U.S. copyright law grants motion picture copyright owners five exclusive rights: to reproduce the work in copies, to prepare derivative uses of the work, to distribute copies, to perform the work publicly, and to display the work publicly.[17] Yet film studios have exerted varying degrees of exclusion and access to their holdings since the industry's origins. Eric Hoyt's *Hollywood Vault* charts the economic significance of American studio film libraries since the rise of the star system in the 1910s, wherein movie fans "sought access to the old films of their favorite stars, preceding critics as proponents of old film screenings. In the 1910s and 1920s, most critics believed that rapid developments in the art of film rendered most old movies inherently inferior to new ones," and it would seem that studios agreed, having subordinated their film libraries to "more pressing goals of gaining market share and maximizing ticket sales in the studio-owned first-run theaters."[18] However, studios changed course during the postwar recession by "defensively using libraries as profit centers . . . [as] the innovations of intermediary television distributors created a new business model, one that deployed libraries aggressively as foundations for the expansion of an entertainment corporation's reach." In the 1940s, the demand from both audiences and critics for old films underwent a distinct shift, moving "from the fringes of fandom toward the mainstream."[19] Through the 1970s, a growing number of film enthusiasts owned 16mm projectors and scoured mail-order catalogs for the "relatively small number of available Hollywood features"—yet despite the rise of nonprofit and small-gauge alternatives, most Americans "encountered old films while attending commercial movie theaters," which often ran revival screenings, "and, later, while watching television. These audiences participated in the commercial marketplace for film libraries, demanding that business buyers obtain specific types of old movies."[20]

A major paradigm shift in media access occurred when Sony began selling its Betamax videocassette recorder in 1975, which Sony Corporation of America president Harvey Schein dubbed a "Xerox for television."[21] This effectively drove film consumption away from the public sphere of movie theaters and into the privacy of one's home, freeing television viewing from broadcast schedules. Viewers could record their favorite films and shows, building a market for the democratization of film reproduction and exhibition. That same year, the FBI raided businesses and seized film prints that had been distributed by Budget Films, a licensed subdistributor for major Hollywood studios, and it was the first time that criminal charges were brought against individuals for film and television piracy. Though Budget was a legitimate film rental company, it was not authorized to sell film prints, which it had done with copies of films such as *Paper Moon* and *The Take,* often to private individuals for their own film libraries (most notably *Planet of the Apes* star Roddy McDowall, who had procured several films in which he'd appeared), and much of its business was directed toward clients in South Africa. In a landmark case, Budget owner Al Drebin was sentenced to "three months in prison and a fine of $20,000, plus three years' probation, making him the first individual to be sentenced to serve time for piracy."[22]

Despite these ongoing battles, the reality of piracy has remained marginal to film history, regardless of its target or method of access. As a commercial form of public entertainment, films can reap economic rewards only if they are publicly accessible; yet, as McDonald writes, "it is only possible to place economic value against that availability if mechanisms of exclusion are used to create artificial scarcity." As a result, "the business of moving images is forever locked into the dialectic of access and exclusion."[23]

However, while studio film libraries have been tampered with or neglected by their corporate owners, nonprofit film archives have stepped in to intervene, most notably in the case of the original National Film Preservation Act of 1988 (NFPA). As Brian Real detailed in this journal, NFPA was drafted in response to the increasing trend of colorization of black-and-white films, "concerned with the preservation of original motion picture content without significant visual alterations."[24] Following this, owing to advocacy by the Library of Congress, film archivists, and other allies, subsequent laws following the initial act were shaped into an "effective public policy plan that provides strong federal support for the physical preservation of motion pictures," including the establishment of the National Film Registry and the National Film Preservation Board (NFPB) and the National Film Preservation Foundation (NFPF). This also served to guide preservation priorities for noncorporate archives "away from a focus on commercially released feature films and toward the preservation of orphan works."[25] Moreover, NFPB "met its goal of increasing the amount of overall funding for film preservation beyond limited federal funds, as dozens of individual and corporate supporters have donated [to NFPF] since 1997."[26] And though many institutional beneficiaries of NFPF are "larger, well-known archives—such as the Library of Congress and George Eastman House—the presence of smaller, lesser-known recipients, including numerous state historical societies [and nonprofits], shows that the foundation successfully publicized its grants and reached out to organizations with films well outside the mainstream . . . [and] confirms a continuing dedication to works without significant commercial potential."[27]

Despite the heroic work of film archives and foundations in advocating, preserving, and protecting film heritage, a great many studio and independent films have never been commercially released on home video or streaming in the United States. Some of these have found a second life as individual video copies or "rips" that are taken from a physical source, uploaded by an individual user, and shared through private networks by enthusiasts. Often, these files were bootlegs taken from original sources, such as television broadcasts or telecine video dupes, and are characterized by low-quality interlaced digital video, owing to older compression standards and the need to be downloadable over low-bandwidth internet connections.[28] The Library of Congress's *Sustainability of Digital Formats* guide notes that

> the largest number of moving image files encountered on the Web or, for that matter, on DVDs and other disk media, have been derived from pre-existing or newly created television signals. When such a video stream serves as the source, then the resulting digital file inherits the source's aspect ratio and maximum possible picture size, as well as the form of the frame scan, i.e., interlaced or progressive.[29]

The high-definition era of streaming video-on-demand content and digital media (i.e., Blu-ray) has favored progressive scans over interlaced, resulting in the introduction of 720p, 1080p HD, and 4K formats. Within pirate film networks, these files are sometimes sourced from region-coded Blu-ray releases or geo-blocked streaming platforms, and for those who live outside those countries and do not own region-coded Blu-ray players, and who cannot access traditional archival holdings, these files are the only way to view these films.

For Enrico Camporesi, a curator at the Centre Pompidou in Paris, the proliferation of copies comes down to a matter of individual use. In discussing the Pompidou's online curation of artists' moving image work during the pandemic, Camporesi writes that "[film's] importance is directly linked to the infinite nuances that are discernible in the ways we use copies, and the goals that motivate such uses." When audiences are unable to travel to the movie theater or the museum to see the work as intended, these "reproductions have to be praised for their use value—and the discussion should then shift to distinguishing not only the good copy from the bad copy, but the virtuous use from the improper one."[30]

PLEX: A PERSONAL MEDIA ARCHIVE

If making a rare film freely available can be construed as an act of virtue, such an act can also become a product of convenience. In recent years, a variety of platforms have emerged that host these files, some of which are highly exclusive, and others of which are operating in plain sight. Plex, an app that hosts personal media collections and is free to register and use, combines exclusivity with a startling ease of access. Essentially, Plex allows users to sync their collections of video, audio, or photographic media files from a hard drive onto a server and to invite other designated users (who must create an account) to access them across a network at their leisure. Plex then delivers the media through the app on one's laptop, phone, or TV. In this way, the website essentially functions as a do-it-yourself streaming platform, with the host providing or restricting access to users as they see fit. A Plex server can host hundreds of movies on it, depending on the size of one's hard drive and internet speed. When one uploads a film to the Plex app, it fetches descriptive metadata automatically from the user-edited site the Movie Database (MDB). Though it sometimes tags films erroneously or mislabels them, users can go through and customize or "match" metadata fields to preexisting MDB records, cataloging their collections as they see fit. Plex can also catalog films through an impressive variety of metadata categories, so one can view them by director, year, genre, and so on. However, where Plex excels in cataloging collections, it lacks in providing other context or any kind of personal recommendation algorithms, outside of retrieving Rotten Tomatoes scores.

The Plex app has existed quietly since 2009, but its subscriber base has increased rapidly over the last several years, from 15 million users in 2019 to a reported 25 million in 2021,[31] suggesting that a generation of increasingly online users have caught on. But while one could share the entire run of an out-of-print show like *Homicide: Life on the Street* alongside a 1080p leaked file of Christopher Nolan's *Tenet,* ready to cast to a friend's TV and smartphone, it is unclear to what extent the company takes responsibility for its fluid and unregulated servers. An article by Bijan Stephen in *The Verge* in 2019 examines this

> main tension of using Plex: while the software itself is explicitly legal, the media that populates its customer-run servers is not—at least the stuff protected by copyright law. The company, of course, doesn't condone this particular use of its software. A spokesperson provided a statement that read, in part, "Plex supports content creators and does not condone piracy," before directing me to its terms of service page.[32]

Whereas websites like YouTube use content identification systems to allow rights holders to monitor unauthorized distribution, Plex does not currently have such restrictions, allowing users to upload and play copyrighted video files as they wish.

Stephen interviewed several users in the *Verge* piece about their Plex habits, which speaks to the extremes to which users can take advantage of the service, claiming that these servers can "function a little like secret societies or private clubs." One user speaks of belonging to a "contingent" maintained over the last decade by a few accounts with servers of thousands of movies and TV shows that are shared to several hundred users and that "rarely gave out . . . coveted invites." But the purpose, Stephen writes, is to "simplify the experience of streaming media and make it feel human. Every Plex server's media catalog is different. They go beyond licensing agreements (because piracy) and anonymous algorithmic curation (because a person is choosing what's on there) to make the streaming experience personal." For many, Plex creates a sense of shared community around media objects, and it functions as an "off-label use that doesn't necessarily feel illegal."[33]

On December 21, 2020, the Protecting Lawful Streaming Act of 2020 was quietly passed into law as part of the Consolidated Appropriations Act, a spending bill that included stimulus relief for the Covid-19 pandemic. Authored by the office of Senator Thom Tillis, the law is aimed at "large-scale criminal streaming services" that stream copyrighted material without the permission of the copyright owner but will "not sweep in normal practices by online service providers, good faith business disputes, noncommercial activities, or in any way impact individuals who access pirated streams or unwittingly stream unauthorized copies of copyrighted works."[34] This does not technically include Plex, a free service that only offers a paid subscription for use of its mobile app and access to broadcast TV streams, nor does the bill target "individuals who might use pirate streaming services." However, the bill sets a precedent for how such personal media streaming services might be scrutinized and regulated in the future.

KARAGARGA: UNDER THE RADAR AND THRIVING

If Plex collapses the boundary between personal media collections and streaming access, it must be asked where users access these rare files to begin with. Enter Karagarga (aka KG), a private international file-sharing community that describes itself as "a comprehensive... archive of film and related materials [that seeks] to promote the ongoing sharing, discovery and discussion of international film, theatre, tv [and] literature."[35] The website is only accessible to users by invitation from other members, invitations which are scarce. But if you receive an invite, you have access to hundreds of thousands of rare films, PDFs, audio files, and fan-created subtitles, all of which are shared through a peer-to-peer system—requiring that users upload as much as (or more than) they download to maintain a positive ratio and good standing in the community. As scholar Caetlin Benson-Allott explains, websites like KG are unique from open torrent sites like the Pirate Bay by "articulating specific terms of use—or community guidelines—and polic[ing] the community to ensure member compliance." In this sense, KG actualizes pirate spectatorship as "based on an equivalence economy and not capitalism's value exchanges."[36]

While KG has very strict rules about remaining active and not taking advantage of its shared system, the site also has a strong international focus and does not allow uploads of mainstream Hollywood or Bollywood cinemas—even though its administrators leave the idea of "mainstream" undefined. It is this "tendency toward the difficult and obscure that has made Karagarga so reliable a haven for cinephiles of discerning tastes," as reported in the *National Post* in 2015, which dubbed it "the most exhaustive library of classic, foreign and arthouse films in the world" and publicized its renown within tightly knit circles of film lovers.[37] The site features a "master of the month" category that focuses on a distinct filmmaker or movement and provides a ratio bonus to users who seed those files. KG also requires specific metadata around the technical specifications of each upload, screenshots for quality assessment, extensive description of the file's origins (including who preserved or released it), and a synopsis or quotes from published reviews or journals whenever necessary—making each record widely searchable. Though plenty of context is provided on the page, an active user forum allows for ongoing discussion, recommendations, and requests for new titles.

Although the website has enjoyed a sixteen-year run, its impact has not remained innocuous. In June 2015, the website underwent a prolonged period of downtime, the cause of which remains shrouded in mystery, according to the *National Post*. An anonymous Twitter user named Judex published a statement taking responsibility for the shutdown, claiming to be "a filmmaker and distributor owed huge amounts of lost revenue by . . . [all of the] Karagarga users who had downloaded his work illegally," and he "promised swift retribution to the culpable parties." "Your rapacious pillage of film culture is annihilating that culture," he wrote. "Only the rich and powerful will survive the assault online piracy is inflicting on cultural production today."[38]

But despite its perceived disruption across the film industry, Karagarga still exists and thrives today, much as the independent film ecosystem has shifted and adapted to new forms of exhibition in the virtual age. Though the site offers free access to copyrighted materials, its servers remain invite-only, explicitly operating on an ethics of trust and requiring users to contribute as much as they take from its ever-growing archive. However, it is inarguable that by removing the physical nature from archival materials, websites like KG and Plex explicitly serve to augment their users' perceptions of films as property.

DISTRIBUTION

While websites like Karagarga may be a boon to shrewd viewers looking for films unavailable on DVD or streaming, they also provide access to contemporary world cinema and new home video releases—and the impact such pirate sites have on independent film distributors seeking audiences for specialty releases is considerably more nuanced and complex. Distribution companies have a major impact on the value of cinema in the global marketplace, as each company "classifies and evaluates the potential of films against each other. By making an investment in selected films and helping to shape their profile in the marketplace, the distribution business impacts on the process of value creation and creates hierarchies."[39] At the same time, in her study of film distribution and piracy in the digital age, Virginia Crisp laments the lack of scholarship on independent film distribution compared to that of Hollywood and points out that such companies vary greatly in size and scope: "informal methods of film distribution are not homogenous activities underpinned by a unified set of motivations that result in a similarly predictable set of outcomes." The relationship between pirates and cultural industries is often "constructed as unequivocally distinct and oppositional," when in fact such "pirate" activities should be considered part of the wider social and cultural processes of film distribution.[40]

The author reached out to several prominent art house film companies to determine their attitudes toward ongoing piracy, including Kino Lorber, a prolific international, independent, and classic film distributor whose virtual theatrical exhibition initiative Kino Marquee was introduced and rapidly expanded in March 2020, partnering with more than 150 art house theaters across the country to keep them in business. Wendy Lidell, senior vice president of theatrical distribution, described the piracy of independent and artists' cinema as a "non-issue," as "the masses are not clamoring to pirate foreign language art films. . . . Our audience skews older and the pirates are young folk who know how to do it. It is a bigger issue for the Hollywood studios."[41] Despite the instant availability of Kino titles on their on-demand platform, the company has been able to maintain its relationship with a devoted base of older art house patrons at home. Indeed, in a 2009 study by Smith and Telang about the impact of television broadcasts on piracy and DVD sales, it was found that while broadcasts would increase the appearance of pirated copies online, they also resulted in increased home video sales. This suggested that companies and creative artists "can use product differentiation and market segmentation strategies to compete with freely available copies of their content . . . [and] that giving away content in one channel can stimulate sales in a paid channel if the free content is sufficiently differentiated from its paid counterpart."[42] In other words, pirates and purchasers may well represent two significantly different segments of the film market.

Some distributors actively embrace the niche and, as such, have to contend with piracy on a more regular basis. Grasshopper Film is a New York–based distributor of international art house and independent cinema that often licenses restorations of films that have never been commercially available in the United States, including home video and streaming releases of restorations of the films of uncompromising Jean-Marie Straub and Danièle Huillet. Ryan Krivoshey, founder and president of Grasshopper, recalled that when the company acquired the entire Straub–Huillet catalog, they went to YouTube and issued takedown notices for the many bootleg copies on the site. "We got so many angry emails from people," he says.

> The idea was that we were basically being capitalist pigs for taking down
> free streams of socialist filmmakers, with [radical political] viewpoints and

so on, and how could we do that, of all the films we chose to take down. The irony is that these copies on YouTube were old beat-up VHS dubs, and we had these new restorations. We were also doing this on behalf of Jean-Marie and his team. So there's a disconnect between the idea of film and content being free. . . . It's not right.[43]

As more specialty titles have been made available for streaming in recent years, on websites like Criterion Channel and MUBI, "the barrier has increased to downloading it illegally, and that has shrunk" the amount of pirate activity, according to Krivoshey. But when a pirated copy shows up on an illegal streaming site, there's little recourse for a small distributor. "It's like this annoying buzzing fly that you know is there, and you fight it as much as possible."[44]

As a former video store employee, Krivoshey acknowledged the sense of community that develops from modern forms of bootlegging. "If someone invites you to watch their collection, or a film that they've uploaded—to me that's like the old days of sharing VHS or DVDs. But there are people on [these sites] who just upload everything and invite everybody, so that sense of community dissolves. There has to be that line [drawn] there."[45] At Kim's Underground on Bleecker Street, which closed in 2005, Krivoshey recalled that the owner, Mr. Kim,

> had all of these bootleg VHS copies in addition to studio VHS and laserdiscs. They would dub these tapes in their office, and people would come in just for [those] films that weren't legally available anywhere else. On occasion I'd come into work and there'd be these guys in suits who'd push us behind the counter, with boxes, they'd strip the shelves of these bootlegs and leave after about an hour. A few days later, someone would come from Mr. Kim's office with brand new bootlegs. And that process would repeat on a regular basis.[46]

But with increased viewing time during the pandemic, Krivoshey was struck by "how many films we want to see that aren't available on the major sites. For some of those we've had to go back and get DVDs or Blu-rays online. But there's a certain point where these films won't even be available on DVD or Blu-ray."[47]

IN THE MARGINS

While digital technology has dematerialized the legal and technical terrain of media piracy, the irony, McDonald writes, is that "the legal authority and legitimacy of copyright [has been] opened up to interrogation and contestation." Given that so much "content" is now available for free, the age of "digital natives" has procured "a generation of media consumers unaware, uncertain or unaccepting of the financial compensations that copyright is designed to protect"—and, subsequently, debates have surfaced on what should or should not be considered copyright infringement. More than ever before, the media industry's control of access and exclusion is being held up to scrutiny and dispute, after decades of occupying the moral high ground and proclaiming piracy as a problem to be urgently combated. "In this new climate, such claims are now equally met by voices countering how the powers of the copyright industries must be resisted, and persuasively portraying Hollywood and big media more generally as the real villains."[48]

In a recent polemic, lawyer and former avant-garde filmmaker Brian L. Frye compares copyright owners to landlords, asking whether copyright should still be treated the same as property in the current landscape. "The copyright cops persist . . . [that] copyright owners are entitled to the entire value of the works they create because that's what property means," Frye writes. "If the purpose of property is to encourage efficient consumption, what is the point of property in non-rivalrous goods or, more simply, goods that don't diminish with consumption?" He uses the recent example of the Internet Archive's National Emergency Library, in which hundreds of books were made available online for free and a group of authors complained of lost revenue, shutting down the service. If owners want to treat their copyright like property, Frye argues, they stand to lose more than they gain, given that the copying of work is inevitable. "Real estate requires regular maintenance, while intangible works of authorship require nothing but possible policing. . . . Real estate is far more volatile, as we've seen in recent memory . . . while valuable works of authorship tend to retain their value. So much so that securitization is pointless."[49] In Frye's view, it is not necessarily the value of the work that is diminished when copies occur but purely that of the owner's or shareholder's relationship to it.

In seeking a response to this argument, the author spoke to Mark Toscano, a preservationist of artists' moving image who has a different view on copyright. "There is sometimes a tendency to believe that artists who are anti-digitization or who avoid digital distribution are choosing to be irrelevant. I disagree . . . [as] there's more to the value of a work than its availability or relevance." Toscano, who has been a member of KG for ten years, acknowledges that the difference in quality and format between public exhibition and home viewing has become negligible. The ability to download rare films has allowed him to screen in classes the work of artists to which he may not have had access otherwise, such as European animated short films whose U.S. copyright has lapsed or whose creators have since passed away. But there's "something so uninspiring about hard drives" when compared to the traditional ceremonial or performative aspect of viewing cinematic works as originally intended.[50]

Although Toscano always obtains permission from contemporary artists to screen their work, he spoke of the impact of this changing landscape on artists with whom he works, such as Crispin Glover, who shoots and exhibits on film and refuses to digitize his work, precluding any possibility of bootlegging. Within the broader field of preservation, Toscano has known of situations where films were leaked from private screeners while they were still in progress, which occasionally results in a "productive dialogue" in the KG comments between users on the ethics of uploading and sharing this work. In this sense, there is always a risk whenever loaning films in digital form, which Toscano has sometimes mitigated by suggesting artists send users a Blu-ray copy instead of a file. "Both formats are vulnerable to bootlegging, but with a disc, someone has to make a reasoned decision and effort to copy it; whereas with a file, someone has to make the effort to delete it." Ultimately, however, Toscano believes that "for anything that's noncommercial, different things are at stake—beyond the artists' potential objections, I don't think there's ultimately a negative economical impact, and in fact the work sometimes benefits from this exposure."[51]

Stephen Broomer, a Toronto-based educator, avant-garde filmmaker, and preservationist of artists' cinema, makes 16mm and Super 8mm work that that he uploads to Vimeo for free as "a pressure move, to make sure the work doesn't just disappear." Broomer spoke of colleagues in the avant-garde filmmaking world whose work will get absorbed into an archive or distribution center, never to be seen again; his work existing online has helped him build an audience. In his view, archives like Karagarga can often do a disservice to the work being disseminated. "The idea of canon-building looms so large in cinephilia that this idea of all-access, or building an archive . . . [can] end up superseding what the most valuable gestures are," he said.[52]

Broomer spoke fondly of La Loupe—translated as "the magnifying glass," a Facebook group started at the time of lockdown that serves as a repository for download links for films "without French distributors, 'orphaned' DVD publishers (nonexistent or sold out) or that have remained under the radar."[53] Theorist and critic Erika Balsom, who has written extensively on film and video circulation in the digital era, placed La Loupe on her 2020 top ten list for *Artforum*: "At its peak, *les loupiotes* dumped hard drives full of treasures, posting download links often accompanied by passionate remarks."[54] "I'm not especially troubled when I see [on La Loupe] obscure films by Edward Owens or Marie Menken that are over 50 years old, brilliant filmmakers who should be recognized. But there's a question of what constitutes value recognition," Broomer explained.

If you think about the work, write about the work, create opportunities to show the work, maybe in some official capacity by paying to rent it—those are great things. But when these works are instead just sitting on someone's hard drive . . . it's some kind of victory [to them] that it's there, and it becomes a new kind of prison for work. To have no critical discourse, that's troubling.[55]

On July 12, 2021, Facebook suddenly shut down La Loupe, which an article in the French paper *Libération* called "the end of a miracle."[56]

CONCLUSION

To what extent does piracy entail negative consequences for artists' cinema? For the Pompidou's Camporesi, he writes that "in this realm, viewing copies, leaked or unauthorized, tend to circulate among a very tight network of connoisseurs, mostly people who are entirely aware of what they are looking at"[57]—and who will, given the chance, seek out the true archival object. But can we take for granted that users know what generation of a film or video is in front of their eyes? In a recent interview, archivist Rick Prelinger spoke about the sense of closure or finality that comes with digitization. "[We think] that once a film is digitized it moves into a new realm of accessibility, it becomes part of a novel and more public sphere of which it was not previously a part. This isn't necessarily true. . . . So much depends on the regime and degree of enclosure surrounding the files."[58] What will last, according to Prelinger, is the consideration of archival appraisal and whether these copies will have permanent value. "Digitization is not a one-time affair. . . . We cannot fully anticipate the future uses of records. Accident . . . plays a significant role in determining the survival (and use) of the archival record. We can (and should) privilege what we consider important, but we need to understand the contingencies, prejudices and hierarchies that cause us to privilege certain records over others."[59] The fight between corporate rights holders and advocates of free expression, Prelinger says, is not of primary importance. "I believe that questions of respect—for creators as well as for potential audiences—are longer lasting and much more difficult to resolve than contemporary legal questions."[60]

When we discussed ways in which archives can respond to this changing landscape of access, Toscano distinguished between three tiers of customers: museums and cinematheques, which often or always properly license titles; educators, who are often at the behest of the resources of their institutions; and individuals, who have their own choices to make. It is in this middle group of educators, Toscano explained, where the greatest changes can occur, and it is they with whom archives need to connect in a more meaningful way. He explained that, often because of a lack of resources or awareness, many professors will inevitably screen work in an educational context without obtaining proper permissions or even seeking better quality copies. Should stronger lines of communication open up between archives and educators, the work can be shown in an equitable manner and will help encourage students—the film enthusiasts of the future— toward more frequent and more ethical modes of discovery.[61] As Vincent Longo argued in his piece on model archives,

> having students research in and help build resources from the archive heightens our awareness, as educators, of how gaps in domain knowledge, artifactual knowledge, and archival intelligence restrict access. This recognition opens new possibilities for college educators and archivists to address the gaps in nonspecialist knowledge to facilitate more fruitful engagement with the materials.[62]

To understand the wider implications of access is to no longer take it for granted.

Micah Gottlieb is an archivist and film curator. Born and raised in Los Angeles, he holds a BA from Sarah Lawrence College (2013) and is a graduate of UCLA's MLIS program (2021) with a specialization in media archival studies, where he did research on the landscape of alternative moving image exhibition in Los Angeles. He is the founder of Mezzanine, an independent and art house revival film series based in Los Angeles whose programs are frequently done in collaboration with artists, curators, and other luminaries from specific disciplines. He is formerly the assistant programmer at the Quad Cinema and previously worked in independent film distribution in New York. He currently works at Sony Pictures Entertainment's data archive.

NOTES

1. Chris Anderson, "The Long Tail," *Wired,* October 1, 2004.

2. Abigail De Kosnik, "2021 Will Launch the Platinum Age of Piracy," *Wired,* December 12, 2020.

3. Katie Dowd, "Why Netflix Has Such a Terrible Selection of Classic Movies," *SFGate,* January 14, 2019.

4. Dowd.

5. "CROSSROADS 2020 Program 1," http://www.sfcinematheque.org/video-programs/crossroads-2020-program-1/.

6. "Quibi Is Reportedly in Talks to Sell Its Content Catalog to Roku," CNBC, January 4, 2021, https://www.cnbc.com/2021/01/04/quibi-is-reportedly-in-talks-to-sell-its-content-catalog-to-roku.html.

7. "Quibi Is Shutting Down," *The Verge,* October 21, 2020, https://www.theverge.com/2020/10/21/21527197/quibi-streaming-service-mobile-shutting-down-end-katzenberg.

8. Paul McDonald, "Piracy and the Shadow History of Hollywood," in *Hollywood and the Law,* ed. Emily Carman, Eric Hoyt, and Philip Drake (London: British Film Institute, 2015), 72.

9. Peter Decherney, "One Law to Rule Them All: Copyright Goes Hollywood," in Carman et al., *Hollywood and the Law,* 26.

10. Decherney, 26.

11. Decherney, 27.

12. Decherney, 22.

13. Decherney, 27.

14. Decherney, 27.

15. Decherney, 30.

16. McDonald, "Piracy," 72–73.

17. Eric Hoyt, *Hollywood Vault: Film Libraries before Home Video* (Berkeley: University of California Press, 2014), 7.

18. Hoyt, 3.

19. Hoyt, 9.

20. Hoyt, 10.

21. McDonald, "Piracy," 79.

22. McDonald, 76–79.

23. McDonald, 70.

24. Brian Real, "From Colorization to Orphans: The Evolution of American Public Policy on Film Preservation," *The Moving Image* 13, no. 1 (2013): 130–44.

25. Real, 130.

26. Real, 144.

27. Real, 144.

28. Vincent Tabora, "Progressive vs. Interlaced," *High-Definition Pro* (blog), December 22, 2019, https://medium.com/hd-pro/progressive-vs-interlaced-e18e2924800e.

29. Library of Congress, "Quality and Functionality Factors for Moving Image Content," https://www.loc.gov/preservation/digital/formats/content/video_quality.shtml.

30. Enrico Camporesi, "Digital Pandemic: Programming and Accessing Artists' Film during the Lockdown," *Millennium Film Journal*, no. 71/72 (Spring/Fall 2020): 108–13.

31. Sarah Perez, "Plex Launches a Subscription-Based Retro Game Streaming Service, 'Plex Arcade,'" *TechCrunch* (blog), January 26, 2021, https://tech crunch.com/2021/01/26/plex-launches-a-subscription-based-retro-game -streaming-service-plex-arcade/.

32. Bijan Stephen, "Plex Makes Piracy Just Another Streaming Service," *The Verge*, July 23, 2019.

33. Stephen.

34. Thom Tillis, "Tillis Releases Text of Bipartisan Legislation to Fight Illegal Streaming by Criminal Organizations," December 10, 2020.

35. https://karagarga.in/.

36. Caetlin Benson-Allott, *Killer Tapes and Shattered Screens: Video Spectatorship from VHS to File Sharing* (Berkeley: University of California Press, 2013), 200–201.

37. Calum Marsh, "Karagarga and the Vulnerability of Obscure Films," *National Post*, July 3, 2015.

38. Marsh.

39. Roderik Smits, *Gatekeeping in the Evolving Business of Independent Film Distribution* (New York: Springer, 2019), 2.

40. Virginia Crisp, *Film Distribution in the Digital Age: Pirates and Professionals* (New York: Palgrave Macmillan, 2015), 2.

41. Wendy Lidell, email correspondence with the author, February 16, 2021.

42. Michael D. Smith and Rahul Telang, "Competing with Free: The Impact of Movie Broadcasts on DVD Sales and Internet Piracy," *MIS Quarterly* 33, no. 2 (2009): 321–38.

43. Ryan Krivoshey, telephone conversation with the author, February 24, 2021.

44. Krivoshey, telephone conversation with the author, February 24, 2021.

45. Krivoshey, telephone conversation.

46. Krivoshey, telephone conversation.

47. Krivoshey, telephone conversation.

48. Macdonald, "Piracy," 90.

49. Brian L. Frye, "OK, Landlord: Copyright Profits Are Just Rent," *Jurist*, April 8, 2020.

50. Mark Toscano, telephone conversation with the author, February 13, 2021.

51. Toscano, telephone conversation.

52. Stephen Broomer, Zoom conference with the author, February 25, 2021.

53. Sandra Onana, "Frank Beauvais, les films rares passés à la Loupe," *Libération*, July 2, 2020.

54. Erika Balsom, "Erika Balsom on the Best Films of 2020," *Artforum*, https://www.artforum.com/print/202009/erika-balsom-84343.

55. Broomer, Zoom conference.

56. Didier Péron, "Le groupe Facebook des films introuvables fermé: la fin d'un miracle," *Libération*, July 13, 2021.

57. Camporesi, "Digital Pandemic," 113.

58. Sophie Cook, Beatriz Bartolomé Herrera, and Papagena Robbins, "Interview with Rick Prelinger," *Synoptique* 4, no. 1 (2015): 185.

59. Cook et al., 186.

60. Cook et al., 186.

61. Toscano, telephone conversation.

62. Vincent Longo, "Model Archives: Pedagogy's Role in Creating Diverse, Multidisciplinary Archival Users," *The Moving Image* 19, no. 1 (2019): 63–74.

Documented Aliens

*Encyclopaedia Britannica's
Revolutionary Foreign-
Language Instruction Films
of the Post-Sputnik Era*

GEOFF ALEXANDER

In response to the success of Sputnik by the USSR in 1957, the United States Congress launched the National Defense Education Act (NDEA) a year later, appropriating more than US$1 billion to be spent over seven years to promote educational development. Science and math were two of the three areas of instruction most prominently targeted. Modern foreign-language instruction, emphasizing the importance of cultural understanding within the linguistics curriculum, was third on the radar screen.

By 1961, Encyclopaedia Britannica Films (EB) had created and released the most comprehensive foreign-language curriculum to date, also being the first to use film as the core educational element. Focusing on French and Spanish (Castellano and Mexican), its use of film, coordinated with textbooks and audiotape, revolutionized foreign-language instruction in schools. Foreign-language instruction prior to the EB series treated moving pictures as little more than supplements to textbooks. Curriculum in the EB series, on the other hand, was driven by film, the teacher's manual emphasizing that students see each film three times prior to opening the textbook to view the script.

Competing film companies, recognizing the prohibitive costs of creating such a series, largely left the field to EB. Today, films, textbooks, and tapes from EB's landmark instruction films of the early 1960s have all but disappeared. Recently, the Academic Film Archive of North America digitized a number of these films, including those discussed herein, for viewing on the Internet Archive.[1]

Seen today, the films unveil cultures in a time warp. Made in France, Mexico, and Spain, they reveal old-world customs meeting head-on with the 1960s, introducing modern dating and a shrinking world impacted by affordable automobile travel. They have ethnographic value, documenting centuries-old customs in danger of disappearing in an increasingly modern world. In these time capsules, actors smoke cigarettes, sport high-fashion dresses, and drive sporty cars—now classics—traffic jams being absent compared to today's congested urban streets.

By the late 1970s, these 1960s-era films had vanished from American school systems, almost completely disappearing from educational film libraries. It's something of a miracle any survived at all. They were the 120-part Je Parle Français, the 54-part La Familia Fernández, and the 27-part Emilio en España series, 191 films in total.

In a departure from the manner in which foreign languages were taught previously, the EB series consisted of video-audio-lingual instruction (VAL), a multimedia term coined by EB Films president Charles Benton, in which 16mm sound films drove the curriculum, supplemented with textbooks and audiotapes. Each series was based on a continuous narrative, characters reappearing throughout each series' films. Made by seasoned directors, they featured professional actors and extensive use of historical places as sets. Characters' development evolved as series films progressed, unveiled by cultural nuances and linguistics. The film series fulfilled foreign-language requirements for three years of study in secondary schools or two years at the university level.

The man behind the films, Croatian-born EB producer Milan Herzog (1908–2010), spoke seven languages, his résumé including stints as a broadcaster for Voice of America, a journalist, a lawyer, a judge, and a schoolteacher.

Figure 1. Filming *Le Mont Saint-Michel* (1961), from the Encyclopaedia Britannica series Je Parle Français. Margot, played by Ghislaine Dumont, is at a restaurant, writing a letter describing Mont-Saint-Michel while lunch is prepared. Local citizens and tourists investigate and walk onto the set. Producer Milan Herzog, wearing a white hat in the left of the frame, included it all in the film. From Encyclopaedia Britannica Inc.

Fifty-two years old when he began filming the first of the series, Je Parle Français, in 1960, Herzog "distinctly remembered" Archduke Ferdinand's assassination in 1914 discussed at the family table in Sarajevo the day it occurred and would live to the age of 101.

NDEA's goals for foreign-language instruction were "effective communication and cultural understanding," the latter element no doubt driven by increasing Soviet international influence. It mandated a clear break from previous methods used to teach foreign languages in schools, codified by its student objectives:

1. To understand a foreign language when spoken at normal speed on a subject within the range of the student's experience.
2. To speak well enough to communicate directly with a native speaker on a subject within the range of the student's experience.
3. To read with direct understanding, without recourse to English translation, material on a general subject.

Figure 2. Crew and cast filming in the countryside for the film *Chaumont* in the Je Parle Français series. Annick Jorré Allières is in the white dress; others are unidentified. From Encyclopaedia Britannica Inc.

4. To write, using authentic patterns of the language.

5. To understand linguistic concepts, such as the nature of the language and how it functions through its structural system.

6. To understand, through the foreign language, the contemporary values and behavior patterns of the people whose language is being studied.

7. To acquire knowledge of the specific features of the country or area where the language is spoken (geographic, economic, political, etc.).

8. To develop an understanding of the literary and cultural heritage of the people whose language is studied.[2]

EB's foreign-language instruction films focused on the study of a civilization based on its language, textbooks emphasizing cultural nuances seen, but not explained, within the film dialogue, keyed specifically to the film in the series where they first appear. A page from the *Je parle français* textbook relating to film 4, *Ma soeur Anne,* explains elements of French culture behind the dialogue:

A. French people consider you "mal élevé" (badly brought up) if you say "Bonjour" or "Au revoir" without using *Monsieur, Madame,* or *Mademoiselle* after them. It is part of their idea of politeness that you greet or take leave of each person individually, calling him by title . . . or by his first name *(Bonjour, Pierre)* if the person is his friend. It is not bad manners in English

Figure 3. Actors Jean Landret and Ghislaine Dumont during the filming of *Le Mont Saint-Michel* in the Je Parle Français series. From Encyclopaedia Britannica Inc.

to say "Hello," "How do you do?" or "Goodbye" without adding a term of address like "Sir" or "Mrs." Nor is it bad manners in German, Spanish, or many other languages. So this custom is typical of French culture, and it must be followed.

B. When greeting each other, French people usually shake hands. In the film of lesson 4, you recall that everyone shook hands when greeting and when taking leave. It may be added that the French handshake is brisk and short, unlike the vigorous "pumping" of American handshakes.

C. Although you may find French students simply saying "Salut" when meeting each other, greetings and leave-takings are very formal among the French. Americans, in comparison, are very casual and will greet each oth-

er with a small hand-wave, a "Hi" or a "Hello." Two Frenchmen meeting on the street will most likely stop, shake hands and exchange formalities.

D. You may have noticed in the film of lesson 4 that the French people did not use the family name of the person to whom they were speaking. They treated the person addressed as though, for the moment, he or she were the ONLY *Monsieur, Madame,* or *Mademoiselle*. And in fact, in the Middle Ages, when the French language and forms of politeness were

developing, it would have been impudent to say "Monsieur Lebrun" to one's feudal overlord, implying that one had more than one such loyalty.[3]

FRENCH REVOLUTION IN FILM: THE 1961 JE PARLE FRANÇAIS, PREMIER DEGRÉ SERIES

Producer Herzog recalled the genesis of the series:

> This French Language project was [one of] the largest single productions Britannica ever undertook—120 lessons on film, with dozens of actors and travel to a variety of locations over at least half a year. Even the origins of the project are unusual. We heard at a convention that a French teacher at a small Ohio college founded by French Huguenots used film to train military officers in French before they were sent to posts in Algiers. It was a complete immersion course. I went to investigate and saw Professor Rosselot teach and heard her students speak. The film she used was her personal creation—very clever but amateurish. I was fascinated and persuaded our management to finance a much expanded French language project. Professor Rosselot took a year's leave of absence, and I became the producer of the series in France with a French crew.[4]

LaVelle Rosselot, prime educational consultant and curriculum developer for the film project, descended from a family arriving from France in the late nineteenth century, settling in southern Ohio. Rosselot's father was a history professor at Otterbein College, her brother Gerald one of the founders of the Scientific Atlanta technology company. She wrote the dialogue for all 120 films in the series and made at least one appearance on-screen, as herself, in lesson 7, "Pouvez-Vous Me Dire?"[5]

Filming began in 1960, made by a crew selected by Tadié-Cinema's André Tadié, noted for his earlier work as a cinematographer on Jean Mitry's 1949 documentary *Pacific 231*. Herzog, who first worked with Tadié during a series of

Figure 5. In the film *Fête folklorique* (1961) from Encyclopaedia Britannica's Je Parle Français series, actors Ghislaine Dumont and Jean Landret (at left) meet traditional dancers from Bretagne, who perform a round dance, accompanied by a chanter and bagpipes. From Encyclopaedia Britannica Inc.

Figure 6. Actors Ghislaine Dumont (far left) and Jean Landret (facing her), with unidentified crew members, shot at Clédon, Finistère, Bretagne, during Encyclopaedia Britannica's Je Parle Français series. From Encyclopaedia Britannica Inc.

Figure 7. Je Parle Français
producers Milan Herzog
(pictured) and André Tadié
compiled a master chart
detailing elements of the 120
films in the series, including
location, décor, actors,
directors, dialogue, and set
equipment. Courtesy Shanta
Herzog.

films on the medieval world filmed for EB in the 1950s, appreciated Tadié's ability to manage the challenges of assembling cast and crew:

> I worked with André Tadié whom I met after the war when he ran a film studio in Paris.... He also knew how to deal with the French unions. In the film industry— as well as other industries—the unions then were dominated by the Communist Party. They had no sympathy for American capitalist directors. There were continu- ous negotiations about employing crew or working conditions for extras. The un- ion leaders were more accommodating because we were making a documentary instead of a feature film and we always managed to find a solution for our prob- lems.[6]

The sixteen crew members, including cin- ematographers Georges Strouvé and Jacques Duhamel, were led by directors Herzog, Pierre Malfille, and Guy Jorré, whose wife was among the principal actors. Filming occurred in sixteen French localities, including Paris; the chateaux of the Loire, Versailles, and Bretagne; and Lake Geneva, Switzerland. Herzog filled a large wall chart with each of the 120 scenes, blocking them out when completed. Cast and crew trave-

led by chartered bus on an extended circuit through France. He improvised: dolly shots of country scenes were taken from a camera popping out of the rear roof of a Citroën "deux-chevaux" automobile. He utilized his actors, most of whom took time off from other jobs, only when he needed them. There were sixty-two speaking roles requiring precise adher-ence to the script, already in preparation for textbook printing. One cast member died on the set; another broke her leg in an auto accident and was subsequently filmed sitting behind a table or with legs obscured by foliage. The film-ing was completed in eight months, with thirty hours of French audiotapes produced as well.[7]

From a historical perspective, the films are compelling cinematic works depicting the France of 1960, most notably cultural rites in Bretagne. Automobile traffic, by today's standards, is practically nonexistent. The films

Figure 8. Producer Milan Herzog (second from left) and actors Jean Landret and Ghislaine Dumont (fourth and fifth from left) during the filming of Encyclopaedia Britannica's Je Parle Français series in 1960 (others unidentified). Courtesy Shanta Herzog.

include contemporary fashions and automobiles (e.g., the haute couture dress worn by the wife in the *Chaumont* film and her arrival at the chateau in a Simca Aronde 1300 Deluxe coupe) and family members smoking cigarettes. The story line encompassed the travels through France of Anne (Annick Jorré Allières), her friend Margot (Ghislaine Dumont), and Margot's uncle (Jean Landret), acting as her guide. Chantal Caffin De Lagrange, Colette de Varga, and François Truffaut veteran Claude Mansard rounded out the six principal players.[8]

A number of films are worthy of comment. *Chaumont* (film 67), filmed at the famed chateau on the Loire, begins with a home scene, the husband enjoying a cigarette. His wife sporting a high-fashion dress, she and Anne tour the grounds after the French style, in fashionable pumps rather than comfortable walking shoes. *Le Palais de Versailles* (film 84) makes little use of language in detailing the interior of the palace, the camera unveiling the Hall of Mirrors, Louis XIV's bedchamber, and numerous interior details, ending with hollow footsteps echoing below the grand staircase. The films *Carcassone* (film 119) and *L'Abbaye* (film 51) provide exceptional cinematic documents of Carcassone and Mont-Saint-Michel. *Le Mont Saint-*

Michel (film 52) features tourists and locals ambling through a local restaurant, curiously eyeing the camera and Ghislaine Dumont while a chef whisks eggs for a meal. Each shot of the monument is elegantly framed while Herzog, as in the other series films, celebrates adding local people to the action, rather than framing them out. The folkloric films of Bretagne are among the most fascinating in the series. *Le pardon* (film 64) documents the Benediction of the Sea festival, with traditional dress and music and a sequence of the blessing of the fleet of fishing boats. *Fête folklorique* (film 65) introduces a parade in Bretagne, with bagpipes, festive dress, and round dances, while *Les funérailles* (film 63) features a traditional funeral.

The series documents city and country

Figure 9. John W. Oller created
the curriculum and textbooks
for Encyclopaedia Britannica's
La Familia Fernández and
Emilio en España series.
Courtesy John
Oller Jr.

life. In *Le camping* (film 117), young women
ride bicycles to a picturesque bluff overlook-
ing a small vineyard, the castle of Carcassone
in the distance. They unload camping equipment, cook dinner, pitch the tent, and settle
down for the night in perhaps the most idyllic
film in the series. In *La ferme* (film 114), niece,
aunt, and uncle drive to visit friends at an old-
world country farm. Producer Herzog briefly
appears in *La tour Eiffel* (film 81), enjoying a
coffee with a female acquaintance. Colette de
Varga as Hélène makes the comment that although he and his companion are speaking
French, they're certainly Americans, evidenced
by his poor pronunciation of the letters *u* and
r in French.

Released in 1961 in black and white as
well as Eastmancolor, each Je Parle Français
film was ten minutes or shorter in length. Texts
included hardbound teacher and student books
as well as a three-hole-punched paperback
student workbook. Two pedagogical films for
teachers, *Teaching French with Films, Pt 1: Lis-
tening and Speaking* and *Teaching French with
Films, Pt 2: Reading and Writing* (dir. Irving
Rusinow) were released in 1966 and 1967, respectively, featuring consultant Alain Favrod
discussing the curriculum in French. LaVelle
Rosselot emphasized the primacy of film as an
immersion learning tool in her introduction to
the 1961 student textbook:

You will be taught in French, not in English. Your object is to understand the film
in French, not to translate it. Translation
at this stage of language learning is NOT
an effective technique. Train yourself immediately to suppress the desire to find
English meanings. . . . You didn't need another language to help you learn English.
You're just as intelligent now as when you
were two or three years old! Don't use a
crutch in learning your French.[9]

After the initial printing in 1961, textbooks
were revised in 1962, 1965, 1968, and 1969.
Magdeleine Tadié, wife of producer André
Tadié, taught the course to foreign students in
France as late as 1967, doubtless contributing
to the revisions.[10] Filmstrips were added to the
curriculum in 1968 or 1969, produced by Margaret L. Wood and Alain M. Favrod, with assistance from consultants Rosselot and Edward F.
Wilgocki Jr.[11] The 1969 *Je parle français premier
degré "nouvelle edition"* teacher's manual and

student text ended with lesson 33. It's unknown whether the curriculum stopped at that point or continued to lesson 120, as before.

In 1971, EB introduced Je Parle Français Deuxième Degré, a secondary-level course consisting of twenty new films, filmstrips, and tapes. Films were classified as either dialogue or cultural films, the former directed by Robert Guez, the latter by Jorré, with Herzog credited as the executive producer working again with the Tadié-Cinema crew. With Rosselot's illness and subsequent death, Favrod supervised the project; Anne Benson and Jean Canolle wrote the scripts.

In 1974, the Je Parle Français Deuxième Édition Premier Degré series of twenty films replaced the 1961 program of 120 films. Wilgocki served as executive producer of the revised series. He arrived at EB in 1967, along with consultant, author, and filmstrip producer Favrod, a fellow French teacher at Abington (Pennsylvania) Senior High School and now project manager of the revised edition. The films were produced by Herzog, filmed through the facilities of Tadié-Cinema, and were directed by Michel Beaudry, Michel Boyer, Jean Goumin, and Jean Leduc, with Alain Maes writing the scripts.[12]

Why was the 120-film series of 1961 replaced? Clothing fashions changed, and smoking cigarettes and celebrating funerals probably caused concern among EB executives. Favrod offers another perspective:

> The revisions became necessary because language teaching methodology had evolved and some aspects of the first edition needed updating. In addition, new filmstrips and a workbook were added to the materials. . . . I remember spending 8 months in France supervising film production and new audio tape recordings.[13]

With the arrival of the new series, the previous curriculum was deaccessioned by educational authorities in favor of a cinematic curriculum shortened from 120 to 20 films, the 1961 series relegated to a historical footnote. One major difference in the updated series was the inclusion of thematic material relating to another racial group with ties to French culture. In director Jean Leduc's *Une recette d'abidjan*

(film 20), an African couple from the Côte d'Ivoire (heretofore aka the Ivory Coast; the name was officially changed in 1985, https://www.un.org/en/about-us/member-states/cote-divoire) hosts their friends, a Frenchman, an Englishman, and a German woman, in their Parisian apartment, cooking a native meal. The Frenchman, formerly a teacher in Côte d'Ivoire, brings a 16mm projector and a home movie to the dinner, showing a film on cooking, industry, and educational sequences (an algebra class) from Côte d'Ivoire, narrated by the guest. The friends become so caught up in discussing the culture of the Côte d'Ivoire that the dinner is burned beyond hope and they repair to a Parisian restaurant specializing in Côte d'Ivoire cuisine.

The 1974 series was fated to have a brief run itself, as Favrod described:

> I know that EB decided to get out of foreign language materials' production at some point. When I was still there, I was already hearing rumours about how exorbitant the development of these materials were. Marketing also was not very happy about having to bring in pedagogical consultants to close sales because the language teaching methodology was such a departure from the book and audio tapes oriented materials. Teachers were very uneasy about having to use film projectors in their classrooms. I don't think EB ever marketed the series of films in VHS.[14]

After the French-language curriculum was dropped, five films from the 1971 Je Parle Français Deuxième Degré series remained in EB's 16mm catalog, listed as the La France Contemporaine series in French and Life in Modern France, its English version. The 1961 films, composing what may be considered an encyclopedic tour through early 1960s France, vanished from schools by the end of the 1970s. The final relics may be the dozens of films from the series found behind a door in Herzog's garage after his passing in 2010.

ENCYCLOPAEDIA BRITANNICA FILMS SPANISH-LANGUAGE INSTRUCTION SERIES

The success of the 1961 French series brought immediate requests for a similar series in Spanish. EB president Warren Everote took the suggestion of district manager Lucien Harrison to hire John W. Oller (1918–80), an instructor in the Fresno, California, school system who wrote a narrative-based Spanish curriculum, to take on the role of building one for EB, to be produced by Herzog and directed by Irving Rusinow (1914–90). Filmed in 1962 with the cooperation of Mexico's Department of Education, fifty-four films, along with audiotapes and textbooks, were produced for the elementary-level La Familia Fernández series, released in 1963.[15] John Oller was a man of adventure. A fluent Spanish speaker, he studied Russian at Princeton and Dartmouth and was recruited by U.S. authorities to spy on Nazi activities in Spain during World War II—his cover, an Argentinian playboy. Followed on the street and realizing his cover had been blown, he incapacitated his tracker with an elongated metal flashlight used as a weapon and was spirited out of Spain, back to the United States, through Portugal. After the war, he ran a cattle ranch in Oklahoma, eventually moving to Fresno in 1953, where he taught at Roosevelt High School.[16]

Herzog recalled his efforts in getting the cooperation of the Department of Education in Mexico City:

> As I was organizing the production crew and hiring people and scouting locations in Mexico, I was told that I needed to get the permission from the Education Department. The professor that was helping me arranged for me to meet the official in charge. When we were in her office, I turned to the Professor to explain the details, but the lady asked who was in charge and when I said it was me, she said that I should be giving the details. Since I did not speak any Spanish, I was very nervous and was sweating profusely, but using my Latin and French, I made up the language and explained the project in as much detail as I could, the lady listened attentively and at the end of my speech turned to me and speaking in perfect English said that she was very impressed with my effort. The result was that not only did we get a lot of cooperation from the Department, but she also accepted my invitation for dinner.[17]

Written in conjunction with University of Pittsburgh scholar Ángel González Araúzo, the films followed the daily life of Pepito, a young boy, and included a cast of ten actors, several of whom were well known in Mexico or would be in the future.[18]

In 1964, producer Herzog traveled to Spain to make the twenty-seven-film secondary-instruction series Emilio en España, with curriculum written by Oller and Ángel González. This series follows Emilio from the first-level Fernández series as he travels through Spain, visiting his grandfather in Sevilla and Cousin Paco in Barcelona. They travel to various regions in Spain, comparing the differences in Paco's Castellano and Emilio's Mexican Spanish in the film dialogue. The films were coproduced by EB and Ancora Films, in collaboration with the Ministerio de Educación Nacional, España, and directed by Antonio Ribas, believed to be Antoni Ribas i Piera (1935–2007), director of fifteen Spanish feature films. Cinematographer Manuel Rojas's (1930–95) credits included more than 170 commercial films and TV series. Director Ribas and producer Herzog hired an array of well-known Spanish stage, television, and screen actors and at least one Argentinian (Idelma Carlo) to perform in the series. Included in the cast of thirty-one speaking roles were Rafael Bardem (1889–1972) and Matilde Muñoz Sampedro (1900–1969), real-life grandparents of actor Javier Bardem, and Mario Humberto Jiménez Pons, continuing his role as Emilio, from the previous series.[19]

Two films from the Emilio series may be viewed on the Internet Archive. Campos manchegos (film 11) shows traditional farming in La Mancha with mule-drawn wooden plows, manual seeding, and flower harvesting. Emilio and Paco drive away in a Land Rover Series II to an ancient inn once visited by Cervantes.[20] In Molinos de viento (film 12), they operate an ancient noria (water wheel), and they visit a country bakery and then a working traditional windmill, focusing on the mechanisms used in milling flour.[21]

THE LOST CURRICULUM: COLOQUIOS CULTURALES

Encouraged by the success of EB's primary and secondary Spanish-language series, Oller and González developed a third-level program, the twenty-film Coloquios Culturales series. The series emphasis shifted to studying the contrasts between American, Latin American, and Hispanic societies; composition principles and techniques; and exposure to a wide selection of Spanish and Spanish American literature. As with the second-level series, Coloquios follows Emilio as he travels through Spain with his Spanish relatives. As Oller noted in his introduction to the field test book,

> one of the principal objectives of this upper division course in Spanish is the appreciation of the value systems of Spanish speaking people. . . . The sociological, anthropological, geographical and historical backgrounds of the people must become known. . . . The question of "what will Emilio study in college?" becomes "who is he," "what is his reason for being?"[22]

The series was produced in 1965, directed by Ribas in a joint Ancora Films/EB project. A two-volume, paperback, 788-page field test edition was produced in 1967, containing dialogue and exercises. The project ends there, the films never distributed, textbooks never printed. It's unknown whether a field test ever took place. The reasons for the third-level course never reaching fruition are open to conjecture, as Herzog, Oller, and EB management at the time have all passed away.

Favrod wasn't the only EB employee hearing rumors of upper management being concerned about costs associated with the foreign-language instruction programs. Martha González, who managed foreign distribution and sales of EB titles, heard them as well.[23]

Benton and Everote, upper-level executives at EB, and producer Herzog all wrote extensively on their histories at the company, extolling the French and Spanish foreign-language series but failing to mention the demise of the most extensive series of film-based foreign-language instruction ever created. These important cinematic documents, reflecting lives, cultures, and times of early 1960s France, Mexico, and Spain, chronicling a revolution in film-based foreign-language instruction, finally fell abandoned, never recouping the costs associated with making them.

The keys represented by EB's language courses of the 1960s opened the doors to cultures and civilizations centuries older than the fifty states. Left today are only fragments: very few films, fewer textbooks, a box of tapes—capsules now almost completely lost to time.[24]

Geoff Alexander is the director of the Academic Film Archive of North America, incorporated as a 501(c)(3) nonprofit in 2001. He holds a master's degree in education and a bachelor's degree in creative arts, both from San Jose State University, and a diploma in French language and civilization from Sorbonne Université Paris. He has authored four books.

NOTES

Select portions of this article were adapted from *Films You Saw in School: A Critical Review of 1,153 Classroom Educational Films (1958–1985) in 74 Subject Categories,* copyright 2014 Geoff Alexander by permission of McFarland & Company, Inc., Box 611, Jefferson, NC 28640. http://www.mcfarlandbooks.com/.

1. Films from EB's Je Parle Français series may be viewed at https://archive.org/details/academic_films?and%5B%5D=je+parle+francais.
2. John W. Oller and Ángel González, *Emilio en España: el Español por el mundo/segundo nivel* (Wilmette, Ill.: Encyclopaedia Britannica Films Inc., 1966), dedication page.
3. LaVelle Rosselot, Margaret L. Wood, Alain Favrod, and Edward F. Wilgocki, *Je parle français, nouvelle edition* (Chicago: Encyclopaedia Britannica Educational Corporation, 1969), 18.
4. Milan Herzog, interview with Cas Goossens, translated by Hans Harmen Smet, undated (circa 2007), publisher unknown.
5. Eathel LaVelle Rosselot (1912–70) died in a farm tractor accident, according to Milan Herzog in an interview with the author on May 15, 2006. Georges Matoré, dean of the

Department of Language and Civilization, Sorbonne Paris, also acted as a consultant for the series. Referring to the episode featuring LaVelle Rosselot, filmmaker Thomas G. Smith notes, "In lesson #7 (at 18:43), I dubbed the voice of the fellow coming down the stairs carrying a tennis racket, 'Hi Chris, see you later.' The French actor playing the role had a bad accent when he spoke English so Milan used me." Tom Smith, personal interview with the author, June 7, 2013.

6. Herzog, interview with Cas Goossens, translated by Hans Harmen Smet, undated (circa 2007), publisher unknown; the author received the translated interview via director/producer George McQuilkin and has been unsuccessful in tracking down Goossens or Smet.

7. Leo Dratfield, "Milan Herzog: A Man of Many Talents," *Kaleidoscope Review,* April 1980; Milan Herzog, personal interview with the author, May 15, 2006.

8. Production and acting personnel are listed in LaVelle Rosselot, *Je parle français Teacher's Manual* (Wilmette, Ill.: Encyclopaedia Britannica Films Inc., 1961). Claude Mansard appeared in François Truffaut's *The 400 Blows* (1959) and *Shoot the Piano Player* (1960) and in Jean-Luc Godard's *Breathless* (1960).

9. LaVelle Rosselot, *Je parle français Student's Text, Lessons 1–33* (Wilmette, Ill.: Encyclopaedia Britannica Films Inc., 1961).

10. Her teacher's manual is in the collection of the author.

11. At least one other text was never published. "Experimental Structure Drills: A Supplement for Je Parle Français," a 120-page paperback draft used by instructor Magdeleine Tadié in a class she taught at the Centre d'études linguistiques in France in 1967.

12. LaVelle Rosselot et al., *Je parle français deuxième édition premier degré Teacher's Manual* (Chicago: Encyclopaedia Britannica Educational Corporation, 1974), iv.

13. Alain Favrod, email correspondence with the author, January 21, 2021.

14. Favrod, email correspondence.

15. Warren Everote, *My Odyssey: A Life in Educational Media 1946–1971* (Santa Barbara, Calif: self-published, 2013), 154–55.

16. John W. Oller Jr., personal interview with the author, June 12, 2020.

17. Herzog, interview with Cas Goossens, translated by Hans Harmen Smet, undated (circa 2007), publisher unknown.

18. Actors in La Familia Fernández included Horacio Casarín (1918–2005), who played Sr Gutiérrez, a soccer star, and whose wife, María Elena, played Sra Fernández; Mario Humberto Jiménez Pons as Emilio (he won the Silver Ariel Award for Best Juvenile Performance at the 1957 Ariel Awards in Mexico for the film *El camino de la vida* [Alfonso Corona Blake, 1956]); and Rodolfo Landa (1926–2004), who played Sr Fernández and was an actor/producer, born Rodolfo Echeverria, who appeared in Luis Buñuel's 1955 film *Ensayo de un crimen* and was the brother of future Mexican president Luis Echeverría. René Dupeyrón, who played Pepito, later appeared in *The Wild Bunch* (1969) and *Bring Me the Head of Alfredo Garcia* (1974), both directed by Sam Peckinpah.

19. Oller and González, *Emilio en España,* 6, 29–31.

20. https://archive.org/details/CamposManchegos.

21. https://archive.org/details/MolinosDeViento.

22. John Oller and Ángel González, *Coloquios culturales, Field Test Edition* (Chicago: Encyclopaedia Britannica Corporation, 1967), iv.

23. Martha González, personal interview with the author, January 20, 2021.

24. The films and textbooks described are in the collection of the Academic Film Archive of North America.

Report on Current Film Cleaning Practices and Issues

AMIA Preservation Committee Film Cleaning Workgroup, June 2022

SUSAN P. ETHERIDGE, ANNE GANT, DIANA LITTLE, AND JULIA METTENLEITER

Keeping film clean is one of the most basic actions of film preservation. Small collections may clean exclusively by hand, and larger labs may have various machinery to clean films, but, for the most part, it is taken for granted that cleaning happens as a key component of good archival practice. Perhaps because it is so integral, it is not widely discussed. However, the techniques, solvents, and workflows employed vary widely among labs and archives and thus merit a closer look.

The AMIA Preservation Committee Film Cleaning Workgroup conducted a survey in 2021 to get a sense of this broad practice of film cleaning. We are grateful to the fifty-four participants[1] who answered. Their responses and comments prompted a longer phase of research, a panel presentation of some interesting case studies at the AMIA conference 2022 in Pittsburgh, and this resulting document.

The survey revealed three key areas of concern for organizations. The first area comprises health, safety, and environmental issues: what products are used for cleaning films, and what are practices for protecting the user and the air, land, and water? The second group of questions was about sharing knowledge: What are the best ways to clean certain films? What are best-practice workflows? Maintenance of machines was a third theme, in terms of both daily upkeep and long-term parts replacement and planning, and those questions also addressed the increasingly scarce supply of qualified maintenance technicians.

The AMIA Preservation Committee Film Cleaning Workgroup has responded to some of these questions within this article and also discovered how little has been written on these subjects. We strongly recommend further research into these topics of concern to the community.

SURVEY RESULTS

Our survey found that 40.7 percent of respondents did not have access to film cleaning equipment.

For those whose employing institution owned a cleaner, the overwhelming majority owned a Lipsner-Smith, with 77 percent of respondents reporting use of that brand. The other brands (CTM Debrie, Kodak, Photomec) were evenly shared across the remaining 23 percent.

Expense (36 percent) was cited as the primary reason for not having a cleaning machine, followed by logistical reasons (23 percent) and lack of knowledge (19 percent).

When Do Organizations Clean Their Films?

One hundred percent of the respondents cleaned films before digitization or duplication, although 68 percent did it immediately before scanning, and the rest did it in preparation for scanning.

Twenty-two percent of the respondents cleaned films before projecting them. Thirteen percent also cleaned films as part of their lending operations. Cleaning, in most organizations, is closely linked to preservation work like duplication or digitization. Possibly because of the time, expense, and additional handling involved, cleaning does not seem to be a priority during the accessioning and cataloging phase that precedes long-term storage but rather happens when a film is taken out for active preservation or screening.

What Cleaning Products Are Most Frequently Used?

The range of answers to this question was broad and reflects the continually changing options and regulations around these chemicals as new ones are created and old ones are discontinued or banned from the workplace. Further discussion follows. Isopropyl alcohol is still the leading liquid (46 percent of users) and is used in both hand cleaning and machine cleaning. HFE 7200/8200 is next in popularity, with 29 percent of users employing this modern

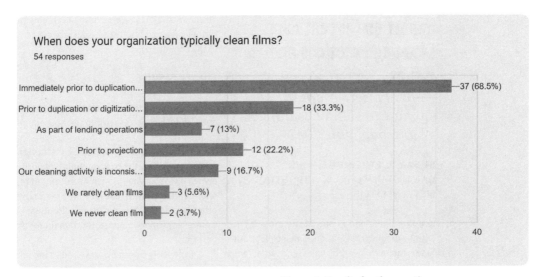

When does your organization typically clean films?

54 responses

- Immediately prior to duplication... — 37 (68.5%)
- Prior to duplication or digitizatio... — 18 (33.3%)
- As part of lending operations — 7 (13%)
- Prior to projection — 12 (22.2%)
- Our cleaning activity is inconsis... — 9 (16.7%)
- We rarely clean films — 3 (5.6%)
- We never clean film — 2 (3.7%)

Figure 1. Results for the question "When do organizations clean their films?"

solvent. Eighteen percent of users are cleaning with perchloroethylene and 18 percent with FilmRenew. In many cases, labs use more than one solution, depending on the cleaning needs and the type of film being cleaned.

In the long view, a variety of solutions is being used, ranging from well-documented noxious chemicals to new products specifically marketed for film cleaning to household products not commonly seen in archiving: Solvon, Vitafilm, Goo Gone, 1-1-1 trichloroethane, UN 1280, Kodak Photoflo, Reliance Specialty Film Cleaner, Film Guard, Tetenal Graphic Arts Cleaner, Fluosolv, van Eyck, and hexane, to name several.

What Cleaning Solutions Have Been Replaced?

Eleven of the respondents have discontinued using perchloroethylene, and 1-1-1 trichloroethane has been discontinued in seven organizations. Other organizations listed isobutyl benzene, FilmRenew, Freon, and HFE 7200/8200 as solutions they have discontinued. This does not mean that other respondents have continued to use these; rather, they may have never used them. This part of the survey, in particular, generated many questions for us, about both the safety of the cleaning solutions and practices and protocols surrounding safe workplaces.

The primary reason given (57 percent) for discontinuing solutions was regulations or a legal requirement, for instance, new environ-

mental laws. Concerns about health and safety came next at 28.5 percent, and 14 percent of respondents changed products because of availability.

These initial findings helped the workgroup pinpoint areas of interest for the archival community. Although each of these topics deserves much more research, following are our preliminary findings in the areas of machine maintenance, hand cleaning, health and safety, and environmental concerns. We have also included two case studies of novel solutions: for a cleaning machine and for a carbon capture system.

CLEANING MACHINE OPERATION AND MAINTENANCE

Cleaning machines vary in size, with full-immersion cleaners generally having a larger footprint than spray or roller-only systems. A small film cleaner may fit on a tabletop, whereas an ultrasonic machine weighs several hundred pounds and will require its own room or corner of a room. Depending on the solvent employed, air exchange must also be considered, even if the machine appears to be well sealed, for the health of operators. Power supply needs (amperage, voltage, and

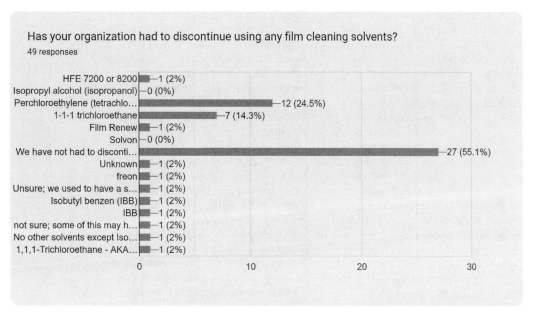

Has your organization had to discontinue using any film cleaning solvents?
49 responses

HFE 7200 or 8200	1 (2%)
Isopropyl alcohol (isopropanol)	0 (0%)
Perchloroethylene (tetrachlo…	12 (24.5%)
1-1-1 trichloroethane	7 (14.3%)
Film Renew	1 (2%)
Solvon	0 (0%)
We have not had to disconti…	27 (55.1%)
Unknown	1 (2%)
freon	1 (2%)
Unsure; we used to have a s…	1 (2%)
Isobutyl benzen (IBB)	1 (2%)
IBB	1 (2%)
not sure; some of this may h…	1 (2%)
No other solvents except Iso…	1 (2%)
1,1,1-Trichloroethane - AKA…	1 (2%)

plug type) vary by model and country of origin.

Service requirements vary widely between cleaner brands and models, but any machine with moving parts will require regular maintenance. A cleaning machine's operation manual should include a maintenance schedule and troubleshooting suggestions. Archive or lab staff can perform most machine upkeep, and it is recommended to have a maintenance schedule for those operating the equipment, including roller changes, reclaiming solvent, and keeping the machine itself clean. Troubleshooting may require a deeper knowledge of electronics or engineering, and the manufacturer will probably need to handle major repairs. This is becoming a concern for many archives, reflected in the survey responses, as knowledgeable technicians, and even manufacturers, are quickly disappearing.

Film cleaner consumables can include filters, buffer rollers, and other cloth elements, in addition to the solvent that is specific to the machine. Perchloroethylene machines might require additional consumables like calcium chips and resin, which can only be sourced from the manufacturer or specialty industrial suppliers. Facilities that strive to minimize downtime may choose to keep spare parts, such as drive belts and capstan rollers, in stock.

Solvent reclaiming is the process by which used solvent is captured and distilled and/or

Figure 2. Results for the question "Has your organization had to discontinue using any film cleaning solvents?"

filtered for reuse. A film cleaner's solvent reclaim capabilities are worth considering, both because of the cost of cleaning fluids and for environmental responsibility. Full-immersion ultrasonic cleaner manufacturers recommend reclaiming solvent in the tank on a schedule that may be based on hours of operation. Running a reclaim operation can take from one to several hours, and the need to reclaim solvent becomes more frequent when cleaning very dirty film.

Solvent availability and cost contribute to the expense of owning a film cleaning machine. Isopropyl alcohol is very easy to find, even at the 99 percent concentration recommended for cleaning film, because it has many industrial and health care applications. Small quantities can be purchased quite inexpensively. As of May 2022, Kodak charges US$640[2] for the five-liter (1.32-gallon) containers of HFE-7200 used with its P-200 Film Cleaning System, and the machine's brochure estimates that five liters of solvent will clean approximately fifty thousand feet of film. These containers are refillable, so solvent can be purchased in larger quantities to take advantage of bulk pricing. Perchloroethylene, HFE-7200, and isopropyl alcohol are all available in thirty- or fifty-five-gallon drums, at least in the United States, for institutions that can afford to purchase larger quantities. Purchasing a film cleaner means committing to a particular solvent, as none of the commercially available machines can accept a different type of cleaning liquid without significant modification. In an update from December 2022, the U.S. manufacturer 3M[3] announced its plan to discontinue production of PFAS chemicals by the end of 2025. In the official statement, 3M mentioned several reasons for this decision, among them the changing regulations designed to reduce or eliminate PFAS in the environment. PFAS (per- and polyfluoroalkyl substance) is a group term for more than ten thousand substances used in a wide range of applications that includes HFE.[4]

Survey respondents commented that contemporary, less hazardous solvents, namely, HFE-7200 and isopropanol, are not as effective at cleaning film that is particularly dirty or oily. There seems to be a trade-off between cleaning efficacy and safety, at least anecdotally. Respondents may be suggesting that "they don't make 'em like they used to" when considering the solvents perchloroethylene and 1-1-1 trichloroethane that were so commonly used to clean film in the past—but perhaps that is not a bad thing. Our priorities have changed as we have learned more about the long-term effects these chemicals have on humans and the environment.

Respondents also cited various maintenance and performance issues with the cleaning machines in their institutions. Some respondents referred to quite specific mechanical or electrical problems that plague them, because of either the expense of parts and service or an inability to enlist help from technicians outside the institution. Other respondents reported very little difficulty in maintaining their cleaning systems, which could be due to the relative age of the machines and/or the size, staff, and maintenance budget of the institutions where they reside.

Some cleaning machine manuals have been scanned and uploaded by their owners to the internet, where they can easily be found. However, some of these machines have been around for decades, and their design may have changed significantly over versions and generations. Ensure that the manual matches the exact model number of the cleaning machine. Manufacturers should be able to provide digital or hard copy manuals to current and potential owners, even for legacy machines.

FEATURED CASE STUDY: DIY CLEANING MACHINE

One DIY machine is located at the Swedish Film Institute (Figure 3). It is a customized water-based cleaning machine constructed by an independent technician from Stockholm. The machine employs an aqueous solution to which a degreasing solvent and Photoflo are added during the different baths. Cleaning the film with water causes its gelatin layer to swell and therefore can reduce scratches while removing oil and dirt efficiently. The Swedish Film Institute only cleans viewing print material with this machine, not original negatives or preservation materials. On one occasion, this machine was used for recovery cleaning after flooding occurred in another Stockholm-based archive facility. This machine has advantages in its facility for cleaning dirty and oily projection prints better than other cleaning machines, its ability to reduce some scratches, and its use of cleaning solvents that are less hazardous for human health and the environment than other solvents (e.g., perchloroethylene). On the other hand, disadvantages include the high water consumption, which may not be environmentally sustainable, and the lack of access to service from the provider.

HAND CLEANING AND NON—MACHINE CLEANING

The cleaning method used depends not only on the film material[5] and its physical condition but also on the availability of in-house equipment and the budget for outsourcing services. Nearly half of the survey participants (41.5 percent) replied that they did not have a cleaning machine within their institution. This number seems to correspond to the fact that more than half of the respondents were working in smaller (zero to ten employees) archival or nonprofit film-holding institutions. Smaller institutions are likely not equipped with an in-house digitization or restoration facility and hence won't

Figure 3. DIY cleaning machine. Copyright Swedish Film Institute, 2022.

have the need to use a professional cleaning machine on a regular basis. In these cases, hand cleaning or cleaning with smaller equipment, like particle transfer rollers (PTRs), is a common practice.

Sixteen respondents stated that they would perform hand cleaning on a daily basis or at least several times per week. Besides being a labor-intensive and time-consuming activity, hand cleaning can carry health and environmental hazards. Solvents used for hand and spot cleaning are often the same as those used in professional equipment, for example, isopropanol or perchloroethylene. Because trichloroethane and perchloroethylene, which are highly hazardous for human health, have been subject to stricter regulation, institutions have looked for safer alternatives. Initially, n-propyl bromide (nPB or 1-bromopropane) was used by some organizations as an alternative cleaning solvent,[6] but in 2010, n-propyl bromide was also designated a higher-hazard substance (RY2016) under the Massachusetts Toxics Use Reduction Act.[7] Suggested replacement solvents from vendors for n-propyl bromide

either have not been tested on motion picture film material or had unacceptable results, causing damage to the tested material.

Other hand cleaning solvents named by survey respondents included hexane, the UN 1280 film cleaner, and Graphic Arts film cleaner. Other degreasing solvents (often available in regular hardware or department stores) not specifically made and tested for film material have also been frequently used by archives and labs. Some institutions have cleaned with these chemicals for decades, because users have observed no damaging or decomposing effects on film over that time period.

In recent years, environmentally friendly options, such as eucalyptus and other essential oils, have found their way into archives and labs to use for spot cleaning. It should be pointed out, though, that the materials safety data sheet[8] (MSDS) for 100 percent eucalyptus globulus oil indicates that the substance can cause skin irritation and allergic skin reaction

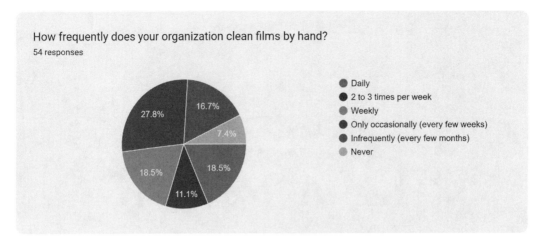

How frequently does your organization clean films by hand?
54 responses

- Daily
- 2 to 3 times per week
- Weekly
- Only occasionally (every few weeks)
- Infrequently (every few months)
- Never

16.7%
7.4%
18.5%
11.1%
18.5%
27.8%

Figure 4. Results for the question "How frequently does your organization clean films by hand?"

and may be fatal if swallowed or inhaled. It is therefore important to use eucalyptus oil only in well-ventilated areas, to avoid contact with the eyes and skin, and to wear protective gloves and safety glasses during use. A study on the effects of manual cleaning with essential oils on the material components of motion picture films has recently been conducted by Caroline Figueroa Fuentes in the master's study program in conservation and restoration of audiovisual and photographic heritage at HTW Berlin (University of Applied Sciences). Preliminary results of this research were presented within the film cleaning panel at the AMIA 2022 conference, and a more comprehensive publication is planned for spring 2023.

Survey respondents also mentioned PTRs and Drypur cleaning rollers as alternative cleaning tools. PTRs have the disadvantage of not being very efficient at removing oil, adhesive residues, or embedded dirt, but they can reduce dust while winding a film.

HEALTH AND SAFETY

Survey results suggest an urgent need for answers and clarity on topics relating to health and safety. When asked what health and safety procedures and personal protective equipment organizations use for film cleaning, the most frequent replies from the survey included the donning of solvent-resistant gloves, protective masks and glasses, as well as having well-ventilated work areas available. Routines for those employees working with cleaning equip-

ment and solvents included staff briefings and training on how to handle cleaning solvents safely, as outlined by the health and safety executive, along with occupational health monitoring or staff rotation systems designed to restrict the time spent working with hazardous solvents.

For many of the fluids used in cleaning, MSDSs are available and should be on file in the space where the machine is being used.

The Film Cleaning Workgroup would like to call special attention to the hazardous nature of trichloroethane, also known as perchloroethylene or perc. This chemical has, for many decades, been used primarily in dry cleaning and textile processing and as a vapor degreasing agent in metal cleaning operations. It is also widely used in ultrasonic film cleaning machines because it is noncombustible[9] and therefore safer to use than alcohol. Over the past decades, perc has replaced 1-1-1 trichloroethane, also known as trichlor, partially because trichlor was proven to damage the ozone layer.

Despite its widespread use, perchloroethylene has been known to have negative health effects on those who come in frequent contact with it. Short-term physical effects from high-level inhalation exposure can include irritation of the upper respiratory tract and eyes, as well as kidney dysfunction. The short-term neurological effects from exposure to the solvent include reversible mood and behavioral changes, coordination impairment, dizziness, headaches, drowsiness, and unconsciousness. Chronic long-term inhalation exposure can cause neurological effects, such as impaired cognitive and neurobehavioral performance. A study published in 2010 stated that people exposed to perchloroethylene had nine times the risk of developing Parkinson's disease.[10] By comparison, the use of hexane, a solvent that is used to clean film by hand, does not increase the risk of the disease, though hexane presents other health risks.

Perchloroethylene exposure can also have adverse effects on the liver, immune system, hematologic (blood) system, and reproduction system. Studies of exposed workers have found associations with several types of cancer, including bladder, non-Hodgkin lymphoma, and multiple myeloma.[11] Because of this, the U.S. Environmental Protection Agency has classified perchloroethylene as likely carcinogenic to humans.[12]

Because of the health and safety risks of perchloroethylene, the Occupational Safety and Health Administration (OSHA) in the United States indicates that the permissible exposure limit (PEL) for perchloroethylene is one hundred parts per million (ppm) over an average of eight hours. OSHA also states that peak exposure should not exceed two hundred ppm for five minutes in any three-hour period. The PEL in California and some other states is twenty-five ppm.

Because perchloroethylene is heavier than water and oxygen, it lingers on the ground. This property increases the hazard to workers who perform maintenance and repair on film cleaning machines, because such work tends to happen at the bottom of the machine. The molecular weight of perchloroethylene is 165.83 g/mol, while water's molecular weight is 18.01528 g/mol and oxygen's is 31.9988 g/mol.

Adequate ventilation must be provided to employees who work with perchloroethylene. If adequate ventilation is not available, a NIOSH respirator must be worn. In confined areas, a self-cleaning breathing apparatus must be worn. "A system of local and/or general exhaust is recommended to keep employee exposures below the Airborne Exposure Limits. Local ex-

haust ventilation is generally preferred because it can control the emissions of the contaminant at its source, preventing dispersion of it into the general work area."[13] If the exposure limit is exceeded, workers should wear a "supplied air, full-facepiece respirator, airlined hood, or full-facepiece self-contained breathing apparatus."[14]

Aside from inhalation, perchloroethylene can also easily be absorbed into the skin. Workers should wear appropriate chemical-resistant gloves when operating a film cleaning machine. A nearby eyewash station is also advised. In addition, employees may want to wear chemical safety goggles or a full face shield where perchloroethylene splashing may occur. Protective chemical-resistant clothing may also be worn, but that is dependent on the potential exposure conditions (such as large spills).

Despite precautions, spills may still occur. When a spill occurs, workers should don necessary personal protective equipment, such as chemical-resistant gloves and/or clothing. If a small spill occurs, workers should isolate the spill and stop its source, if it is safe to do so. Workers can absorb the spill using inert media and place the soiled media into a suitable container (airtight and leakproof). If a large spill occurs, workers should shut off or plug the source of the spill as long as it is safe to do so. They should dike the area to contain the spill and salvage as much liquid as possible into a suitable container. Any residual liquid should be absorbed onto inert media and placed into the suitable container. The perchloroethylene should not be allowed to enter a drain, a sewer, or any waterway.

The following first aid measures are for perchloroethylene. A person suffering from acute exposure to inhaled vapors should immediately be moved to fresh air. If they are not breathing, give artificial respiration, and if breathing is difficult, give oxygen to the person. Call a physician. If a person has ingested perchloroethylene, *do not induce vomiting* but instead give large quantities of water. Never give anything by mouth to an unconscious person. Perchloroethylene is an aspiration hazard.

If a person's skin comes into contact with perchloroethylene, the person should immediately wash with soap or a mild detergent for at least fifteen minutes. Any contaminated clothing and shoes should be removed and washed before being worn again. As with inhalation exposure, call a physician.

If a person's eyes come into contact with perchloroethylene, they should immediately flush their eyes with plenty of water for at least fifteen minutes while lifting their lower and upper eyelids occasionally to allow water to rinse the entire eye. Medical attention should be sought immediately.

ENVIRONMENTAL ISSUES

Hazardous waste[15] poses a greater risk to the environment and human health than nonhazardous waste and therefore requires strict control. Not all but some film cleaning solvents, for example, perchloroethylene, are classified as hazardous waste. In addition, packaging waste that contains hazardous substances is also considered hazardous waste and, like perchloroethylene, requires special disposal. Even if a cleaning solvent is not classified as hazardous, it may still be necessary to arrange for disposal only through organizations that specialize in hazardous waste.

State laws and regulations govern disposal of hazardous waste, which is often managed by local waste disposal authorities. Therefore specialized and licensed treatment, storage, and disposal facilities should be contacted to obtain professional information about disposal for hazardous wastes.

The solvent 1-1-1 trichloroethane, also known as methyl chloroform, is a popular solvent previously used as a film cleaner. It is clear, colorless, nonflammable, and nondamaging to film. Its use decreased rapidly after the signing of the 1987 Montreal Protocol on Substances That Deplete the Ozone Layer, a global agreement that sought to protect the ozone layer by phasing out substances that damaged it. The agreement went into force in 1989, and use of the solvent was banned in 1996, with possible use exemptions.

Over the years, perchloroethylene has become a popular replacement for 1-1-1 trichloroethane in film cleaning machines. Like 1-1-1 trichloroethane, perchloroethylene is clear, colorless, and nonflammable. It is one of the most widely found substances in hazardous

waste sites in the United States. The solvent is mostly released as vapor directly into the air. When perchloroethylene gets into surface water or surface soil, it tends to evaporate quickly. However, it can potentially leach below surface soil into groundwater and the air space between soil particles, thus contaminating them.

A hazardous waste disposal company should be employed to get rid of unwanted perchloroethylene. Because it is a soil and water contaminant, perc should never be poured down a drain or onto soil. "Federal regulations prohibit land disposal of various chlorinated solvent materials that may contain tetrachloroethylene [perchloroethylene]. Any solid waste containing tetrachloroethylene must be listed as a hazardous waste unless the waste is shown not to endanger the health of humans or the environment."[16]

FEATURED CASE STUDY: PACKARD HUMANITIES INSTITUTE CARBON CAPTURE SYSTEM

The film lab at the Packard Humanities Institute (PHI) in Santa Clarita, California, takes precautions in its use of perchloroethylene and the operation of its cleaning machine to be as safe as possible to both its staff and the environment.

PHI uses a carbon capture system from Evoqua Water Technologies, the Vent-Scrub Adsorber VSC 200, to capture perchloroethylene vapors from the cleaning machine. This system is ideal for a small organization or lab (Figure 5).

The carbon capture system consists mainly of a steel drum containing two hundred pounds of carbon that is attached to the bottom of the cleaning machine and an exhaust fan at the top of the drum. The carbon acts as a scrubber for the perchloroethylene fumes, and the small amount of remaining fumes goes through the exhaust fan via a tube that leads outside the building. Before the perchloroethylene vapors enter the carbon drum, the concentration of perchloroethylene is approximately three hundred ppm. After the vapor is scrubbed, the concentration can be as low as one ppm—far below the California and OSHA PELs.

As the vapor enters the exhaust tube, it is measured with a handheld photoionization gas detector or "sniffer." When the sniffer reads

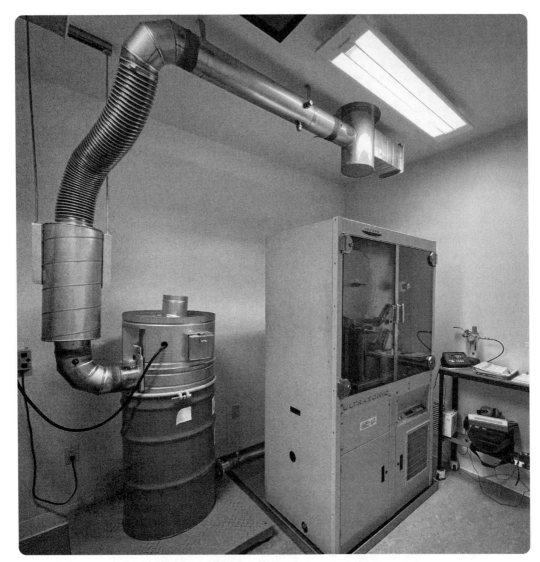

Figure 5. PHI carbon capture system.

approximately five ppm, that is when break-through is about to occur—when the carbon is saturated and can't scrub as well as it did when it was first attached to the cleaning machine. When the reading is ten ppm or higher, the drum is changed.

The carbon capture system can absorb an average of five gallons of perchloroethyl-ene vapors before the carbon is saturated and unable to scrub as well as it did when it was new. Approximately forty thousand to fifty thousand feet of film can be cleaned per gallon of perchloroethylene. It is important to note that the carbon can still absorb perchloroethylene after breakthrough, but not nearly as well as it does prior to breakthrough.

CONCLUSION

Film cleaning practices seem to be a matrix of suboptimal solutions. Some options take a great deal of time or are technically demanding. Some options present health hazards, or they may be too expensive. Each practitioner must weigh the trade-offs between time, safety, cost, performance, and maintenance issues to find the best cleaning option for the films, while considering the environment and the humans who are doing the work.

We hope that the survey and this article encourage further investigation into film cleaning in the archival community. During this project, we found many questions that deserve a more thorough review. We would like to know more about the long-term effects of various cleaning methods on films, with special attention to their effects on nitrate, tinting/toning, and stencil films. We would like to know more about the chemical composition of some of the branded and proprietary film cleaning solvents for which no MSDSs were available.

As part of this research, we contacted the Image Permanence Institute (IPI), which confirmed that it has not conducted any kind of research or study on the long-term effects of cleaning solvents on different film base materials.[17]

It may benefit the AMIA community to start user groups for specific cleaning machines, especially as knowledge about maintenance and parts is likely to become more scarce.

As Janice Allen stated in her survey response, "proper cleaning is a very important part of the preservation process and is a step that should not be taken lightly. Film elements need to be cleaned responsibly, as those elements are often the best remaining preservation element, keeping in mind that much of such remaining film elements may very well outlive the digital data being generated from them."[18] Cleaning carefully and thoughtfully, knowing how to avoid damaging the element, is a critical step for long-term film preservation.

GENERAL INFORMATION ABOUT FILM CLEANING

The National Film and Sound Archive of Australia offers a detailed guide to film cleaning[19] in its online *Technical Preservation Handbook,* with specific suggestions for how to spot clean with a cotton swab, information on PTR rollers, and lists of solvents. Brian Pritchard's website also provides a lot of useful information about motion picture film cleaning.[20]

Susan P. Etheridge works as a film technician for the Hearst Newsreel Project: a joint effort between the Packard Humanities Institute (PHI) and the University of California, Los Angeles (UCLA) to digitize 27 million feet of UCLA's Hearst Newsreel Collection. Susan obtained her master's degree in moving image archive studies at UCLA in 2014. Prior to the Hearst Newsreel Project, she worked as a film technician at the motion picture labs Colorlab and Fotokem.

Anne Gant is head of film conservation and digital access at Eye Filmmuseum, Amsterdam, the Netherlands. She is the current head of the FIAF Technical Commission and a member of the AMIA Preservation Committee.

Diana Little directs the Film Department at the MediaPreserve, a laboratory outside of Pittsburgh, Pennsylvania, that specializes in the digitization of archival audiovisual materials. Prior to her time at the MediaPreserve, Diana spent most of a decade working on film restorations at Cineric Inc. in New York City. She holds a bachelor's degree in film production, history, and theory from Vassar College and completed the certificate program at the L. Jeffrey Selznick School of Film Preservation at George Eastman Museum. She currently serves on the board of the Al Larvick Conservation Fund and has participated in Home Movie Days in New York and Pittsburgh since 2003.

Julia Mettenleiter is an archivist and restorer at the archival film collections of the Swedish Film Institute and a current cochair of the AMIA Preservation Committee. In addition to her MA degree in literature and film studies from the University of Munich, she graduated from the L. Jeffrey Selznick School of Film Preservation in 2018. Previously, Julia held the position of assistant project manager at the film restoration laboratory L'Immagine ritrovata and worked for the Il Cinema Ritrovato festival in Bologna, Italy.

NOTES

Thanks to all the survey respondents, and a special thanks to Janice Allen for her extensive information.

1. Participants: fifty-four archives and practitioners responded, with the majority (thirty-nine) from North America, but there were also respondents from Europe (nine), Asia (three), South America (two), and Africa (one). Respondents came from a variety of institutions: some were from large university archives or national archives, as well as a few commercial labs. The Austrian Film Museum, the British Film Institute, Bundesarchiv, Michigan State University, Pro-Tek Vaults, the Swedish Film Institute, the MediaPreserve, the UCLA Film & Television Archive/Packard Humanities Institute, and the University of Toronto were among the respondents.

More than half of the responses (53.9 percent) came from places with fewer than ten employees. The rest of the respondents came from institutions of varying size: ten to fifty employees (twelve respondents), fifty to one hundred employees (nine respondents), and more than one hundred employees (four respondents).

The respondents also came from a range of institutions, both not-for-profit and for-profit, and several identified as self-employed and/or consultants: archival film holding institution (thirty-two respondents), for-profit film preservation company (ten), not-for-profit entity providing film preservation services (six), consultant or self-employed/volunteer provider of film preservation services (four).

2. Per email correspondence with Kodak sales staff.

3. https://pfas.3m.com/pfas_uses.

4. https://www.kemi.se/en/chemical-substances-and-materials/pfas.

5. The cleaning method is mostly dependent on the material (nitrate, acetate, polyester) and also whether the film contains applied color techniques (tinting, stencil or hand coloring, etc.).

6. https://www.turi.org/Our_Work/Policy/TURA_List/Higher_Hazard_Substances/n-Propyl_Bromide_nPB.

7. https://www.mass.gov/doc/complete-list-of-tura-chemicals-august-2021.

8. According to OSHA HCS (29CFR 1910.1200) and WHMIS 2015 regulations.

9. https://www.cdc.gov/niosh/npg/npgd0599.html.

10. Thomas H. Maugh, "Industrial Solvent Linked to Increased Risk of Parkinson's Disease," *Los Angeles Times,* February 7, 2010.

11. http://www.atsdr.cdc.gov/ToxProfiles/tp18.pdf.

12. https://www.atsdr.cdc.gov/ToxProfiles/tp18.pdf.

13. http://www.ciscochem.com/assets/perchloroethylene-sds.pdf.

14. http://www.ciscochem.com/assets/perchloroethylene-sds.pdf.

15. The U.S. Environmental Protection Agency (https://www.epa.gov/hw) has defined four different hazardous waste characteristic properties. "A waste may be considered hazardous if it exhibits certain hazardous properties ('characteristics') or if it is included on a specific list of wastes EPA has determined are hazardous ('listing' a waste as hazardous) because we found them to pose substantial present or potential hazards to human health or the environment. EPA's regulations in the Code of Federal Regulations (40 CFR) define four hazardous waste characteristic properties: ignitability, corrosivity, reactivity, or toxicity (see 40 CFR 261.21–261.24)." https://www.epa.gov/sites/default/files/2016-01/documents/hw-char.pdf.

16. http://www.atsdr.cdc.gov/ToxProfiles/tp18.

17. IPI's executive director confirmed in an email conversation from March 2022 that no research on this topic has been done.

18. Janice Allen, email correspondence with the authors, November 29, 2022.

19. https://www.nfsa.gov.au/preservation/guide/handbook/conservation.

20. http://www.brianpritchard.com/FAOL/contents/260420ofaol/Foncd/TEXTS/sect_6/filmcleaidx6.html.

Book

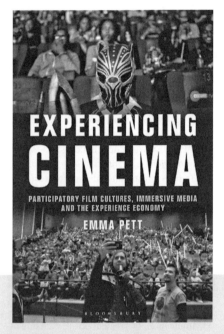

Experiencing Cinema: Participatory Film Cultures, Immersive Media and the Experience Economy
BY EMMA PETT
BLOOMSBURY ACADEMIC, 2021

Hannah Lee

Traditional perspectives of film studies address cinema as a medium, format, or art form with associated scholarly studies in terms of historical, cultural, societal, or literary contexts; in contrast, Emma Pett, in her latest book, *Experiencing Cinema: Participatory Film Cultures, Immersive Media and the Experience Economy*, focuses on active audience participation in cinema. Although the majority of cinema experiences occur with the audience as consumers of what is projected on a screen, Pett explores the different modalities of audience participation as part of the cinematic experience.

Experiencing Cinema divides its titular topic into two parts: part 1, focusing on alternative, commercial cinema experiences, and part 2, concentrating on the "alternative screen experience economy" (2) consisting of activism, rural cinema, and immersive identities through cosplay and crossplay. Initially, the two parts seem to address the potential for commercial success versus noncommercial ventures. The division addresses the motivation of cinema organizers and cinemagoers that leads to deeper themes of cinema as experience, as immersion, and as participation. Pett goes further by asking readers to rethink the "experience economy" of Joseph Pine and James Gilmore (the term first used in their 1998 article "Welcome to the Experience Economy"). Pine and Gilmore argue the need for experiences or events becoming products, a potential economic avenue that becomes a value-added aspect of a product.

As it applies to film studies, Pine and Gilmore's experience economy directly addresses part 1 in its application of commercial immersive cultures that take the cinematic experience to live cinema, pop-up media, and participatory interactions. The first chapter, "Immersive Cinema-going and the Pop-Up Economy," introduces the pop-up cinema landscape in the United Kingdom through the screening of popular films from franchises like Star Wars, Harry Potter, and Back to the Future or themed events around seasonal films like *The Snowman*. Much of these types of pop-up cinema play on nostalgia and the ability to recreate childhood experiences as adults and for a new generation of children. As a result, these events are less about the films themselves and more about the ability to (re)create a sense of community based on themes or fandom. Harry Potter becomes less about Daniel Radcliffe and his acting and more about "shar[ing] a beer with my Potter friend who is also a massive fan, thinking everyone around us felt the same" (41). However, the often higher-than-standard cost of these extra expenses comes with the expectation of an experience to match the price. Although Pett notes that some of her interviewees expressed disappointment, as expectations did not meet the price of admission, she does not delve too deeply into the correlation between the experience economy and the economy of participants' expectations. Instead, the focus becomes more about the cultural aspects of social interactions occurring within these immersive spaces.

The next chapter, "Virtual Reality and Immersive Technologies," switches the focus on people, society, and culture with virtual reality (VR), augmented reality (AR), and mixed reality (MR) experiences. A fairly recent form of technology, virtual experiences are already pushing the boundaries of what is possible as cinematic participation. Perhaps one of the most accessible means of understanding MR is through *Star Wars: Secrets of the Empire*. Building on the success of the Star Wars franchise, *Secrets of the Empire* was released in tandem with the premiere of the film *Rogue One* (Gareth Edwards, 2016). The MR experience allowed participants to engage with the story, making participants active members of the Star Wars universe. Unlike Star Wars, with its established universe and realistic setting, *Draw Me Close* (Jordan Tannahill, 2019) is a stylized, black-and-white line drawing bringing the audience into the creator's artistic universe. Audiences can add to the experience by drawing cats, birds, and other elements. In contrast, *The Deserted* (Tsai Ming-liang, 2017) is voyeuristic rather than interactive. Following a day in the life of one man, the immersion is intimate but "spatially disorienting" (77), as audiences could see and hear but not touch. All of these experiences break down into three

major concepts, according to Pett: the "liveness" (or communication) of an experience, the empathy emerged, and agency or interactivity. *Secrets of the Empire, Draw Me Close,* and *The Deserted* engage with audiences with different levels of liveness and agency capable of spanning the breadth of emotions from these different experiences.

The final chapter of part 1, "Live Installation Art and Participatory Cultures," is a case study of *The Clock* (Christian Marclay, 2010). A supercut of twenty-four hours' worth of clocks and timepieces in film, *The Clock* is not a part of the typical cinema experience with set schedules and (relatively) short run times. As a film, *The Clock* holds a universal appeal beyond the typical art installations, gathering intergenerational and various audiences. In this regard, the film has a way of democratizing art, making it accessible to the masses instead of ticket holders. As a nonticketed event, installations of *The Clock* were based on people's ability to wait in line instead of on cost. As an art installation, *The Clock* allowed museumgoers the opportunity to interact as much (or as little) as they wanted, whether for a few minutes or several hours. The film also forced museums and other art venues to extend their hours to allow visitors to experience the entire film and change typical experiences of both cinema and art studies.

The previous chapters focused on different modalities of film itself, from the environment before, during, and after a film screening to the technology that delivers it to audiences. In contrast, part 2, "Participatory Cultures of Resistance and the Alternative Experience Economy," focuses more on the people and cultures that emerge from these alternative experiences. "Experiencing Cinema in a Rural Context" is one of the best embodiments of the function of cinema beyond the film itself. Pett provides an overview and funding process of cinema for rural areas in the United Kingdom before addressing its two audience groups: the local community and the tourist community. The films screened become secondary to the ability of people to spread out in rural areas to come together and network; it gives reason for individuals to catch up, see familiar faces, and have fun (125). In contrast, tourists can use these rural cinema screenings to have a mini-holiday and explore remote parts of the country, such as castles, lighthouses, and other points of interest throughout the United Kingdom. These rural cinema tourism events are very much similar to the pop-up events from chapter 1, but with a focus more on the location and the local community.

"Cinephile Activism and Rituals of Resistance" shifts focus through examinations of U.K., Bangkok, and Thailand cinema cultures that promote diversity and inclusivity, particularly for feminism, queer activism, and efforts against state censorship. By analyzing the Scalarama festival, Scala cinemas, and independent art houses and theaters, Pett finds trending themes where theaters work with one another (rather than compete for attendees), sharing an enhanced sense of social responsibility.

The final chapter, called "Cosplay, Crossplay and Immersive Identities," is an ambitious examination where individuals subsume the identities of characters in films (and other intellectual property) through Disneybounding, cosplay, and crossplay. Disneybounding is a casual form of cosplay where individuals wear everyday clothes that emulate Disney characters. Although there is no requirement to assume a character's identity, there is a strong connection to the fandom. Cosplay is another step of immersive identity that combines master costume crafting and playacting a character. Most often seen at conventions and other fan gatherings, cosplay becomes a form of live performance, ranging from amateur to expert. Crossplay is yet another step that allows individuals to cosplay characters opposite their genders; the characters they crossplay can also be represented as the opposite gender. The key theme of all these forms of immersive identities is the acceptance of these representations and character embodiments within their respective environments. Disneybounders are capable of hiding their subsumed characters, but cosplayers and crossplayers are accepted within specific environments; dressing and acting as characters in the general public are often met with negative attitudes. Much like films with specific times, locations, and run times, cosplay exists in a set environment of acceptability.

Overall, *Experiencing Cinema* is a strong examination of the different ways people engage with film. One of the many strengths of *Experiencing Cinema* is its ability to combine analysis of chapter themes with the literature and data. While the impact of the global pandemic created by Covid-19 curtailed many of the data-gathering efforts, Pett strengthens her arguments throughout the book by shrewdly applying research methods to the audience community of the chosen case studies. On the other hand, a more formal data methods section with results and analyses would have allowed deeper insights and potential for future research based on Pett's work. Perhaps this could have come from funding that might have assisted Pett with data gathering and other elements of the book.

However, Pett does a wonderful job of incorporating academic analysis and writing for a wider, general audience. It's no wonder that Pett has such insights, with a long history of publishing at the intersection of media audiences and institutions, in addition to her work with the British Board of Film Classification and the Arts and Humanities Research Council. *Experiencing Cinema* is the next step in understanding the concept of "experience" and how it relates to the cinematic landscape. Although it is not a comprehensive text, Pett compiles a series of case studies with quantitative and qualitative data that develops a conversation for past, present, and future studies.

Hannah Lee is the discovery and systems librarian for California State University, Dominguez Hills, with a focus on digital technologies and their social impact. Some of her interests include copyright, intellectual property, cybernetics, book arts, mentoring, and volunteering for nonprofit organizations.

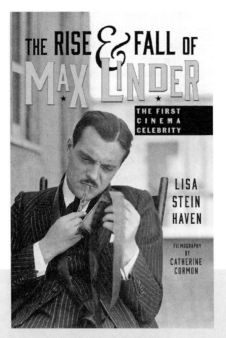

The Rise and Fall of Max Linder: The First Cinema Celebrity
BY LISA STEIN HAVEN
BEARMANOR MEDIA, 2021

Ulrich Ruedel

Film comedy, of course, began with the Lumière brothers' *L'Arroseur arrosé*, and soon, such as with the Cretinetti comedies featuring André Deed, turned into a major and sustainable genre. Yet few film historians would dispute that, owing to the sophistication and characterization he introduced to the formula, Max Linder is the true "father of film comedy" and, with his international success and recognizability, indeed "the first cinema celebrity"—thus the subtitle of Lisa Stein Haven's new biography, *The Rise and Fall of Max Linder.*

Given Linder's significance, the relative lack of literature on the pioneering comic and film star, especially outside of the French language region, is utterly puzzling. There have been monographs in France, such as Charles Ford's small 1966 book and, perhaps most notably, daughter Maud Linder's memoirs, *Max Linder était mon père,* and her lavishly illustrated tribute, *Les dieux du cinéma muet:*

Max Linder, both from 1992. However, a proper biography of Linder, let alone in the English language, has been sorely lacking. Granted, Snorre Smári Mathiesen's 2017 *Max Linder: Father of Film Comedy,* from the same publisher as the new volume discussed here, beat Stein Haven to the market by a few years. However, according to its preface, which kindly acknowledges Stein Haven's then-upcoming work (a favor she returns in her own introduction), it is based mostly on freely available sources, such as online newspaper archives, and also the thorough work of the late Georg Renken of now-defunct maxlinder.de, to whom all scholars and fans interested in Linder are seriously indebted.

With substantial and thorough historic and academic groundwork, Stein Haven's book thus fills a huge gap with a project whose time had come (to paraphrase David Shepard, as quoted in Stein Haven's acknowledgments) and that was encouraged and supported by many a scholar and aficionado, including this reviewer. The author frankly concedes that the work cannot be considered outright definitive, because she was unable to access "the newly formed Institute Max Linder at the Institute Lumière . . . [and] the artefacts and documents portrayed in Maud [Linder's] books and in her films," but this does not diminish its value at all.

As editor of Chaplin's collected *A Comedian Sees the World* articles and author of *Charlie Chaplin's Little Tramp in America, 1947–77,* and as organizer of the 2010 Chaplin Conference in Zanesville, Stein Haven is no stranger to the world of silent comedy. Perhaps most notably, as biographer of the great Syd Chaplin, she has previous experience in chronicling the films, careers, and lives of neglected, talented, troubled funnymen whose film historic impacts have yet to be fully understood. With the same academic rigor and research acumen she has previously brought to the cultural impact of Charles Chaplin and to the life and work of his half brother in the first-ever biography of that major comic, Stein Haven embarks on chronicling the life, films, and career of Linder from his youth to his life's tragic coda.

After tracking the comedian's upbringing, adolescence, and budding stage and film career in "Auspicious Beginnings (1883–1905),"

REVIEWS 106

illustrated with photographs from her own research visits to relevant sites, the author highlights Linder's path to global stardom in "A Screen Comedian (1905–1912)." A quick and concise business history of Pathé sets the stage for the story of Linder's ascent and the creation of his "dandy" character, thus establishing his career as "the first incidence of film-star marketing in history." Indeed, the energetic and strategic engineering of Linder's professional path, in no small part undertaken by himself, takes center stage in the book, throwing new light on the true driving forces behind the comedian's global fame and on the relevance of such ambition in his life. In all this, Linder emerges not just as an immensely successful actor but also as a driven man.

Stein Haven wisely acknowledges the importance of both Linder's films and the stage tours in cementing his stardom (along with a short discussion about his brief excursion into bullfighting). She also puts significant emphasis on the role of newsreel appearances in promoting Linder as a well-known star, referencing a number of these in what are, in essence, filmographic asides throughout the course of the text. Such an insightful exploration of the creation of the comic star image should be more widely explored in the study of visual comedy, because it presented comedians with the challenge of either perpetuating a celebrity image or consistently impersonating their comic character once the newsreel cameras were rolling. Thus Keaton or Laurel and Hardy, for instance, would invariably lapse into their screen characters once the newsreel cameras rolled, though arguably for "dandy" Linder, the perceived difference between celebrity and comic figure may not have appeared as drastic.

The chapter "World Fame and World War I (1913–1916)" explores Linder's Eastern European tour, which included a chance encounter with a young Dimitri Tiomkin. Stein Haven briefly touches on the important history of certain gags, such as the (apparently copyrighted) mirror routine, and addresses the inevitable comparison between Linder's and Chaplin's screen characters, with Chaplin a dominating force since entering film in 1914. In the same period, the reported death of Linder in the Great War was a harbinger of tragic things to come.

Chaplin continues to loom large in "America, the Land of Opportunity (1916–1917)" as the reader follows Linder to the United States to effectively fill the position Chaplin had left at Essanay and eventually take the same path from Chicago to California. The chapter also chronicles the two great comedians' mutual admiration but also what must have developed into a genuine friendship between them. Upon his return to France, Linder's *Le petit café* (1919) is once again, inevitably, framed against Chaplin, here via the 1914 Sennett films *Tillie's Punctured Romance* and *Caught in a Cabaret*. Stein Haven documents Linder's subsequent return to the States in the chapter "America Revisited (1919–1922)," which saw him star in the three well-known American features recently restored and issued in Blu-ray by Lobster Films of Paris. Again, the chapter also substantiates Linder's career progression through his appearances in the "screen snapshot" type of short films and tracks what sadly was to be the final chapter of the Chaplin–Linder friendship.

"Decline and Departure (1923–1925)" tracks the last phase of Linder's life and career, his collaboration with Abel Gance *(Au secours!)*, and his final film, *Le roi du cirque,* both from 1924. However, at the center is Linder's ill-fated marriage to young Ninette Peters, ending in the tragic coda of the murder/suicide of the couple at Linder's hand. It is on this difficult terrain that Stein Haven's matter-of-fact style benefits the work best. She does not mince words in her brief yet powerful evaluation of the shocking events.

While refraining from any couch psychology, and without delving further into this tragedy, it seems only fitting that a brief epilogue, "Court Cases," concludes the book's biographic section and, in doing so, honors the life and work of Maud Linder, the daughter Max Linder left behind, who dedicated her life to reestablishing the great comedian's work. Any research on Linder is indebted to her, as to the late, oft-quoted maxlinder.de founder Georg Renken. Stein Haven adds substantially and, for the first time, comprehensively to these important foundations.

This, however, is not the end of the story, nor of the book. While no doubt there will be future Linder research, the preservation of his films needs to continue building on Maud

Linder's legacy. To support this cause, following the (slightly confusingly placed) index, the book adds a whopping 162 pages of utterly thorough filmography, edited by Linder preservationist Catherine Cormon. While the filmography understandably excludes the aforementioned newsreels as well as "connected films" Linder used in his stage performances, this is no small feat: Linder's entire theatrical film oeuvre is documented in detail by contemporary plot summaries, release dates, lengths, alternate and international titles (including 28mm and 9.5mm reissues), archival holdings, title cross references, and source notes, the last of these once more reminding us of the importance of Renken's research work for his maxlinder.de website, in part thus now further preserved in paper form through its inclusion in Cormon's filmography.

This writer has no doubt that the work of Cormon (and Renken) in this joint volume will rank alongside such extremely valuable reference catalogs as Malthête/Mannoni's *L'Oeuvre de Georges Méliès* or Marie/Le Forstiers's Pathé catalogs, rendering the book as a whole not only a worthy addition to any film studies library, thanks to Stein Haven's biography, but also, owing to Cormon's section, indispensable to film archives in their efforts to unearth and preserve more of Linder's legacy.

Ulrich Ruedel holds a doctorate in analytical chemistry from the University of Muenster, Germany, and worked on optical biochemical sensors and intellectual property rights before turning to the practice and science of film preservation. As a 2005 graduate of the L. Jeffrey Selznick School, he has explored heritage color systems, such as Technicolor, at the George Eastman Museum. Subsequently, he worked as research and development manager at Haghefilm Conservation, as project manager for the nonprofit Haghefilm Foundation, and as conservation technology manager at the British Film Institute before accepting his position as professor for conservation and restoration of modern media (moving image and sound, photography) at HTW Berlin–University of Applied Sciences.

The Greatest Films Never Seen: The Film Archive and the Copyright Smokescreen
BY CLAUDY OP DEN KAMP
AMSTERDAM UNIVERSITY PRESS, 2018

Matthias Smith

In *The Greatest Films Never Seen,* Dr. Claudy Op den Kamp provides several frameworks to understand the challenges that current international copyright law creates for film archives, why these difficulties exist, and how archives (primarily through the example of the Eye Filmmuseum in Amsterdam) should view their holdings, specifically orphan films, as rich resources for both found footage filmmakers and rewriting film history itself. Op den Kamp writes from a deep seat of knowledge—she received her PhD from Plymouth University, as well as degrees in film archiving from the University of East Anglia and in film studies from the University of Amsterdam. Currently she works as a senior lecturer in film and faculty member at the Centre for Intellectual Property Policy and Management at Bournemouth University, United Kingdom, and she previously coedited the 2019 volume *A History of Intellectual Property in 50 Objects* for Cambridge University

Press. Op den Kamp builds directly on previous work in *The Greatest Films Never Seen*; much of the book's content consists of revised and edited selections from articles she previously published in peer-reviewed academic journals.

Throughout her book, the author attempts to make things easier to understand through analogies. The first, amusingly, offers films (particularly orphan films) as akin to the baby in the handbag from Oscar Wilde's *The Importance of Being Earnest*. Hence the handbag represents the archive, holding on to these films, while the "adults" (copyright holders, laws, and bureaucracy) are stuck in a game of formalities. According to Op den Kamp, this reflects archives' historical origins as repositories of films that often find their way there by chance. In previous decades, archives were less likely to be transparent about their holdings, in an effort to avoid the attention of litigious copyright holders. However, as the archival world has moved toward access, and especially digitization, this necessitates a change. The challenge for film archives is that funding is often tied directly to making materials accessible online or digitally. If a film's copyright status cannot be cleared, then it falls into a gray area, unless it has a particular champion.

Utilizing the Eye Filmmuseum as her primary example, Op den Kamp suggests a new categorization for film collections, which maps out the rest of the book. Splitting this map into four quadrants (similar to the "political map" often seen online), the quadrants represent two areas: copyrighted films and films in the public domain. The *x* axis acts as the line between accessible and inaccessible, the *y* axis acts as the copyright barrier, and the four areas are, in order, counterclockwise, (1) films under copyright for which the archive holds rights, (2) films to which the archive does not have rights (third-party copyright holders and orphan films), (3) public domain films that are not accessible (due to processing, rarity, condition, or donor restrictions), and (4) films in the public domain that are readily accessible.

For most archives, the vast majority of holdings are under copyright; Op den Kamp suggests that the average is approximately 70–90 percent. Of these, the majority of the films belong to third-party copyright holders

or are in limbo as orphan films. Although major studios and distributors may work with an archive for screenings or restorations, other copyright holders may be less amenable. Op den Kamp calls this the "Swiss Bank" model of archiving and uses the example of *Als Twee Druppels Water* (Fons Rademaker, the Netherlands, 1963). The film, placed with the Eye Filmmuseum by its financial backer, was rarely made available until the backer's death in the early 2000s, rendering the film mostly as a deposit. The Eye Filmmuseum paid for the film's maintenance, but it was removed from Dutch and international circulation for over thirty years, despite being a critically well-received film upon its original release.

For the orphan film, Op den Kamp provides two separate definitions. The first is a legal one: a film for which a copyright holder cannot be identified or located by someone who wishes to make use of the work. The second is a more theoretical one: if a film is inaccessible, and known only to an archive, it (like *Als Twee Druppels Water*) is removed from film discourse and is "orphaned." In both cases, providing access to orphan films entails risk. If an archive decides to put a film on DVD or otherwise provide access, a copyright holder may appear and then claim restitution. This also hinders an archive's ability to restore certain works, because the archive cannot justify doing so when there is the risk of learning that it cannot provide access to the films due to copyright complaints. While always a concern, Op den Kamp notes that the Eye Filmmuseum has never had a single copyright claim made toward an orphan film in its collective history. Each archive needs to make its own risk assessments, according to its own copyright laws, but the value a film may contribute to either reuse or history must also be considered and not left in the "handbag" of the archive.

For public domain films, Op den Kamp notes that those that can be cleared can easily be made accessible through a network of funds, provided they have someone to champion them. She specifically uses the example of *Beyond the Rocks* (Sam Wood, 1920), which was considered to be a lost classic with notable performers before it was rediscovered in the Eye Filmmuseum. Paramount Pictures, the film's original producer, had failed to renew its copyright over fifty years before and declined to participate in its restoration. However, because the film was free from copyright restrictions, Eye was able to receive grant funding and other resources to restore the film. Had the film still been under copyright to Paramount, it would have likely stayed in archival limbo.

For other films, however, there remain problems related to archives: a critical lack of staff and funding and the ever-common problem of a massive backlog of materials needing care and cataloging. Op den Kamp notes, in closing her book, that the predecessor to the Eye Filmmuseum, the Nederlands Filmmuseum, executed a project to recatalog its entire collection in the late 1980s and early 1990s. This resulted in the rediscovery of countless treasures and oddities that may have otherwise been buried for decades. She makes comparisons to the paper print collection at the Library of Congress and its connection to the Brighton Congress, which gave birth to New Film History. Whereas previous film history relied on scarcity and traditional texts, the Brighton Congress championed the films themselves, highlighted by the surviving paper print collection from the Library of Congress. The paper print collection was born out of a necessity of copyright and an accident of how to accomplish it and was revived due to its public domain status and by those who championed the collection's restoration. Op den Kamp leaves her readers with the challenge that if archives would focus on the aesthetics of their collections (either literally or by what they have), rather than attempting to support established film history and canon with selections from them, this would inspire new uses and discoveries that would bolster individual archives.

For the vast majority of archival workers, whose knowledge of copyright is enough to know what a headache it is, *The Greatest Films Never Seen* offers a refreshing and approachable text. While light on American copyright law specifics, the book's European bias provides a good counterpoint to the more dry and litigious-minded American documents. The book's main weaknesses are found in its origin as a series of separate articles. While Op den Kamp has made a valiant effort to bring her previous work together, the transitions come across as less than smooth, often feeling like welded joints. This is most obvious when certain analogies are presented: Oscar Wilde's handbag vanishes, save for a solitary point, after the introduction. Other idioms, such as the "Power" and the "Swiss Bank," feel vague and aren't as clear when read as a whole (they work better individually, but readers' opinions may vary). They are, however, strongest when Op den Kamp keeps to her quadrants of classification. In tackling the copyright system and archives, Op den Kamp makes a valiant reexamination and a rousing cause to deliver art from the shackles of orphanhood through bureaucracy. And yet the book actually buries at least one interesting solution in its footnotes, in which Op den Kamp mentions the possibility of utilizing blockchains (more familiar today as the identification system for online cryptocurrency) in tracking films when they're processed. This is an extremely fascinating idea that should have been forwarded in the text itself, although the author's reluctance to assign too much emphasis may be due to recent developments in and the popularization of these technologies occurring after she had completed the initial draft of her text, as well as their complicated ethical and ecological challenges.

Despite these small complaints, *The Greatest Films Never Seen* does provide an excellent and creative explanation of the copyright issues facing archives, as well as possible redevelopments of the concept of an archive's response to and engagement with them.

Matthias Smith is a trainee in film collection management at the Eye Filmmuseum. He has an MA in film studies from the University of North Carolina Wilmington. He works primarily on classical Hollywood, queer cinema, melodrama, and archival advocacy.

DVD/Blu-ray

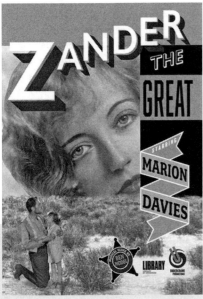

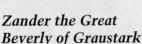

Zander the Great
Beverly of Graustark

DVD/BLU-RAY DISTRIBUTED BY UNDERCRANK
PRODUCTIONS, 2022

Aurore Spiers

Once considered the real-life model for Susan Alexander in *Citizen Kane* (Orson Welles, 1941), Marion Davies (née Douras) (1897–1961) is now enjoying a renaissance among cinephiles and scholars alike. No small credit is due to Ben Model, Edward Lorusso, Crystal Kui, and Marlene Weisman, from Undercrank Productions, who have released six of Davies's silent films over the last five years.[1] With *Zander the Great* (George W. Hill, 1925) and *Beverly of Graustark* (Sidney Franklin, 1926) now available on DVD and Blu-ray, Undercrank Productions continues its admirable mission to rehabilitate Davies as a talented comedienne. The two films are presented on their own, with no program notes or added features, but with new theater organ scores composed and performed by Model.

Produced in Hollywood by Cosmopolitan Productions, and distributed by Metro-Goldwyn-Mayer, *Zander the Great* and *Beverly of Graustark* were vehicles for Marion Davies, a former Broadway showgirl and a rising movie star who excelled at physical comedy. As historians have shown, Davies also served as "actress-manager" of her own production unit within Cosmopolitan Productions, which her married lover, the press magnate and real estate tycoon William Randolph Hearst, had founded in 1917.[2] Even though she was rarely credited for her contributions to screenwriting and casting, for example, several collaborators have confirmed that she often was the driving force behind the production of the films in which she also starred. *Zander the Great* and *Beverly of Graustark* were likely no exceptions.

In *Zander the Great,* which Undercrank Productions presents in a new 2K digital scan made from a 35mm preservation from the Library of Congress, Davies interprets a young woman named Mamie Smith, whose journey from squalid orphanage to blissful home the film follows with sympathy and the occasional touch of humor. Adapted from Edward Salisbury Field's 1923 play by screenwriter Lillie Hayward, *Zander* is composed of two main parts, the first set in New Jersey, the second on a ranch in Arizona.[3] It begins with a change of fortune for Mamie, when Mrs. Caldwell, played by the actress and future gossip columnist Hedda

Hopper, invites the girl to live with her and her son "Zander" (Jack Huff). Mamie then leaves the orphanage, where she has been mistreated, and transforms under Mrs. Caldwell's tutelage "from cabbage to rose." Yet fate strikes again. After Mrs. Caldwell dies, Mamie and Zander are forced to embark on a trip to the West, where they hope to find Zander's long-lost father. Once there, they settle at the ranch of redeemable gang members, one of whom Mamie ultimately falls for. A chase on horseback, a sandstorm, and a last-minute rescue scene ensue before all is well again for Mamie and Zander.[4] The reedition by Undercrank Productions also features a beautiful new theater organ score by Ben Model, one that successfully captures the mood changes throughout the film.

Although *Zander the Great* makes for a pleasant viewing experience overall, the most memorable moments are the comedic ones, when Davies loses control of a bicycle in the courtyard of the orphanage or when she gives terrible haircuts to the gang members at their ranch in the West, for example. We owe these moments, at least according to historians Cari Beauchamp and Jennifer Parchesky, to the woman credited as the film's "editorial director" and better known for her many adapted and original screenplays, Frances Marion.[5] The phrase "editorial director" is somewhat confusing in this context. But Parchesky explains that Marion had a hand in "conceiving the story, co-authoring the script, selecting cast and director, 'suggesting shots and angles,' and negotiating ongoing conflicts between the insecure [director George W.] Hill and the tyrannical [William Randolph] Hearst."[6] A close friend to and repeated collaborator with Davies, Marion strongly believed in Davies's comic skills, for which she apparently advocated when Hearst wished to see Davies in more dramatic roles. As Beauchamp reports, Marion once said to Hearst, "Marion [Davies] is a natural-born comedienne and she is being smothered under pretentious stories and such exaggerated backgrounds that you can't see the diamond for the setting."[7] Davies, too, might have been responsible for the comedy in *Zander,* even though her contributions as "actress-manager," so far, appear to have gone largely unrecorded.

Marion Davies shines even more in the feature comedy *Beverly of Graustark,* which was adapted by screenwriter Agnes Christine Johnston from George Barr McCutcheon's popular 1904 novel with the same title.[8] The film departs from its source in significant ways. Most important is Johnston's decision to have Davies's character, Beverly, impersonate her cousin Oscar (Creighton Hale) when Oscar becomes unable to take the throne of Graustark. As Oscar, Beverly evades a series of murder attempts and experiences various laughable misunderstandings. As herself, Beverly sneaks out in women's clothes (designed by Kathleen Kay, Maude Marsh, and André-Ani) during the night and falls in love with her dashing protector, Dantan, Prince of Dawsberg (Antonio Moreno). When the real Oscar finally makes it to Graustark in time, before Beverly gets discovered, Beverly then resumes her life, with Dantan by her side.

Key to the film's success is Davies's cross-dressing, which becomes the source of many jokes about gender roles and conventions throughout the film. The first example to come to mind is when Dantan fires Beverly/Oscar's escorts and asks them to undress out of their uniforms right away. In a series of medium shots and close-ups, Davies not only conveys Beverly's embarrassment with some brio but also expresses subtle excitement and amusement at the sight of nearly naked male bodies. Another remarkable scene takes place soon after, when Beverly/Oscar arrives at the castle in Graustark. As Dantan and her valet try to get her ready for bed, Beverly/Oscar screams about being "in a man's palace surrounded by men," which several other intertitles, penned by Joseph Farnham, also emphasize afterward. Whereas the valet present in the room smiles at what he interprets to be Oscar's craving for a woman, we the viewers sympathize with Beverly's aspirations to be left alone.

Sporting what came to be known as a "Beverly Bob," Davies—like so many other young actresses in the 1920s—plays the part of a new woman with both beauty and brains. In *Girls Will Be Boys: Cross-Dressed Women, Lesbians, and American Cinema,* Laura Horak tells us that, between 1922 and 1928, approximately ten films were released every year in the United States that featured cross-dressed women.[9] Like Davies, who had already appeared in men's clothes in *Runaway Romany* (George Lederer, 1917), *When Knighthood Was in Flower,* and *Little Old New York,* these women were "almost universally young, slim flappers" starring in historical dramas with lavish sets and costumes.[10] In an article titled "Girls Will Be Boys" from *Picture-Play Magazine,* Davies—in her costume from *Beverly of Graustark*—is featured next to Anna Q. Nilsson, Sally O'Neil, and Leatrice Joy, among others.[11] "In the 1920s," for Horak, "observers connected cross-dressed women to the era's jazzy attitudes and women's new physical and social freedoms," which, I suspect, must have been the case for *Beverly*'s audiences.[12]

For viewers today, the Library of Congress's new restoration of *Beverly of Graustark,* from a 4K digital scan of a 35mm nitrate print in the Marion Davies Collection, is nothing short of a revelation. Besides Davies's performance, most extraordinary is the two-color Technicolor sequence at the end, when Beverly is reunited with Dantan. Screened at the Pordenone Silent Film Festival in October 2019, *Beverly of Graustark* is now presented with a new theater organ score by Ben Model.

The mission is accomplished for Undercrank Productions, whose releases of *Zander the Great* and *Beverly of Graustark* showcase Marion Davies's comic acting skills. As Rob King writes in a previous issue of *The Moving Image,* the work of Model and his team is all the more formidable that it is entirely crowdfunded through Kickstarter campaigns.[13] But the achievement is even far greater from my perspective. Undercrank Productions recovers not only Davies but also several other women—Lillie Hayward, Frances Marion, and Agnes Christine Johnston—whose careers as screenwriters remain either unknown or unnoticed. My only regret is that *Zander the Great* and *Beverly of Graustark* do not include any program notes emphasizing both Davies's status as an actress-manager and these other women's contributions.[14] However, I remain immensely grateful to Undercrank Productions for bringing Marion Davies to the screens in our homes.

Aurore Spiers (she/her) is a postdoctoral teaching fellow and lecturer at the University of Chicago. She received her PhD in cinema and media studies from Chicago in 2022. Primarily focused on women's contributions to cinema, her work interrogates film historiography through the lens of gender and intersectional feminism. Her first book project, based on her doctoral thesis, studies women's labor in French film archives from the 1920s through the 1970s. Her writing has appeared in *1895: Mille huit cent quatre-vingt-quinze* and *Feminist Media Histories.* She is a contributing editor and country coordinator (France) for the Women Film Pioneers Project.

NOTES

1. The other releases from Undercrank Productions include *The Bride's Play* (George Terwilliger, 1922), *Beauty's Worth* (Robert G. Vignola, 1922), *When Knighthood Was in Flower* (Robert G. Vignola, 1923), and *Little Old New York* (Sidney Olcott, 1923). For Undercrank's full catalog, visit its website at https://undercrankproductions.com/.

2. For more on Davies's career, readers may consult Lara Gabrielle's new book, *Captain of Her Soul: The Life of Marion Davies* (Berkeley: University of California Press, 2023).

3. By 1925, Lillie Hayward had written at least one other film for Marion Davies, titled *Janice Meredith* (E. Mason Hopper, 1924). According to the *Moving Picture World* of May 16, 1925, "it was through the advice of her sister, Seena Owen, the screen star, that Lillie Hayward entered the ranks of scenario writers. This was about six years ago, and up to that Miss Hayward had studied to be a professional musician. Her sister's advice, however, proved to be very good, for Miss Hayward immediately showed a special bent for the work." "Brains and Creative Genius Assured by Fox 1925–6 Roster of Scenarists," *Moving Picture World,* May 16, 1925, 335. After a successful career writing silent films, Hayward apparently continued to work in the sound era, for Disney, among others.

4. In *The Times We Had,* Marion Davies discusses a scene from *Zander the Great* where she "had to fight a lion in a lion's cage." Davies, *The Times We Had* (New York: Ballantine Books, 1975), 42. She then explains that "Charlie Chaplin came over and did the scene for me, in my clothes. And that was the first time I ever met him" (43). Yet the extant version of the film presented by Undercrank Productions does not include such a scene. On his blog, Edward Lorusso suggests that Davies might have been confusing two different films. "The Kevin Brownlow Stash," *Silent Room* (blog), April 27, 2018 (no longer available). Indeed, Lorusso once acquired from Kevin Brownlow a still image showing Davies on a set, in front of a cage at the circus. But although it was marked "Zander the Great" in pencil on the side, it probably came from another title. Interestingly enough, a second still image from apparently the same film, yet attributed to *Zander the Great,* also circulates on IMDb, https://www.imdb.com/title/tt0016560/mediaviewer/rm1276409344/.

5. Cari Beauchamp, *Without Lying Down: Frances Marion and the Powerful Women of Early Hollywood* (Berkeley: University of California Press, 1997), 165; Jennifer Parchesky, "Women in the Driver's Seat: The Auto-Erotics of Early Women's Films," *Film History* 18, no. 2 (2006): 174–84.

6. Parchesky, "Women in the Driver's Seat," 180. Frances Marion and George W. Hill later married, in 1930.

7. Beauchamp, *Without Lying Down,* 106.

8. Agnes Christine Johnston was probably considered a good fit to work with Marion Davies because of her success writing for Mary Pickford, whom Hearst wanted Davies to emulate. Johnston also wrote *The Pasty* and *Show People,* both starring Davies and directed by King Vidor in 1928. For more about Johnston, see April Miller, "Agnes Christine Johnston," in *Women Film Pioneers Project,* ed. Jane Gaines, Radha Vatsal, and Monica Dall'Asta (New York: Columbia University Libraries, 2013), https://wfpp.columbia.edu/pioneer/ccp-agnes-christine-johnston/.

9. Laura Horak, *Girls Will Be Boys: Cross-Dressed Women, Lesbians, and American Cinema* (New Brunswick, N.J.: Rutgers University Press, 2016), 125.

10. Horak, 125. *Runaway Romany* was written by Marion Davies herself. It also marked her debut as a screen actress.

11. "Girls Will Be Boys," *Picture-Play Magazine,* July 1926, 91, https://archive.org/details/pictureplaymagaz24unse/page/n597/.

12. Horak, *Girls Will Be Boys,* 126.

13. Rob King, "Review of Undercrank Productions," *The Moving Image* 19, no. 2 (2019): 142–45.

14. Undercrank Productions differs in that sense from Milestone Films, whose detailed press kits for most of its releases constitute valuable resources for curators, scholars, and teachers alike: https://milestonefilms.com/pages/press.

Review Essay

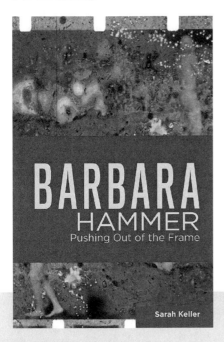

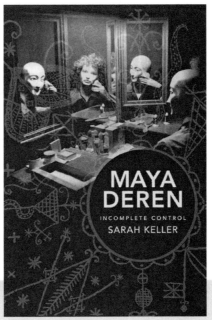

Barbara Hammer and Maya Deren

BARBARA HAMMER: PUSHING OUT OF THE FRAME
BY SARAH KELLER
WAYNE STATE UNIVERSITY PRESS, 2021

MAYA DEREN: INCOMPLETE CONTROL
BY SARAH KELLER
COLUMBIA UNIVERSITY PRESS, 2015

Bart Testa

Sarah Keller has been productively writing on experimental cinema for a decade. While still a graduate student at Chicago, she coedited (with Jason Paul) and introduced the important anthology *Jean Epstein: Critical Essays and New Translations* (2012). Now a professor of art history and cinema at the University of Massachusetts, she has published *Anxious Cinephilia* (2020) and two book-length studies of central women experimental filmmakers. Her latest book, *Barbara Hammer: Pushing Out the Frame*, is the primary focus of this review essay, but it bears a short comparison with

her earlier *Maya Deren: Incomplete Control*. That book ends with a teaser, a short, coda-like discussion of Hammer's filmed homage *Maya Deren's Sink* (2011), shot in the West Hollywood house where Deren made the inaugural film of the American avant-garde, *Meshes of the Afternoon,* in 1943. Though linked deliberately in this way, and intending with her new book to add Hammer to the list of Deren's important heirs, the two filmmakers confront Keller with different critical issues.

When Deren died in 1961, she was already a historic figure. Since then, she has been the subject of decades of scholarship and interpretation. Most writing is aimed at her small corpus of four films made between 1943 and 1946, which is regarded as canonical in avant-garde cinema. Meanwhile, Hammer left behind almost one hundred films in various styles and levels of quality. She turned them out steadily, often four or five a year, over the course of a long career, with her first serious steps in the 1970s and a conclusion coming just a year before her death in 2019. Her strongest arc began with one of her best-known films, the feature-length *Nitrate Kisses* (1992). By then she was already widely famous as "a foremother of contemporary queer experimental cinema" (23). How will Keller deal with Hammer's veritable hoard of movies? How did she deal with Deren's short filmography and the lengthy stretches of incomplete and abandoned films?

There is also a serious difference in intellectual achievement between the two artists. Hammer became known quickly in the 1970s in the Bay Area as a lesbian community filmmaker, with her vibrant, sexy shorts, like *Dyketactics* (1974), *Superdyke* (1975), *The Great Goddess* (1978), and *Double Strength* (1978). Keller writes that this cycle "distinguishes Hammer" and that "they are most frequently identified as foundational for Hammer's legacy to cinema history" (23). Though she was always charming when introducing her work, Hammer produced no serious commentary to go with her films. In contrast, Deren was hailed as a genius who not only reignited experimental filmmaking after the long interregnum following the disappearance of the European avant-garde in the 1930s; she was also the first American to frame a poetics for an artists' cinema with her lectures and writing and especially her *Anagram of Ideas on Art, Form, and Film,* published in 1946 as a chapbook. She was then twenty-nine. A large cohort of filmmakers, scholars, biographers, and critic-interpreters followed her lead well into the 1960s. To add to or break from the extensive published commentary on Deren presents a challenge: the writer would have either to dig deeper into the details of her life or write against the grain and hazard building a new framework. Combining both, Keller manages her new take by making "incompleteness," instead of interruption, the signal feature of Deren's project, and even central to her aesthetics.

If Deren left only a handful of finished films—and Keller counts her output at seventy minutes of screen time—they suggest, in outline, two main genres of experimental film to come: the trance film and mythopoeic films. Her completed film cycle, begun with *Meshes,* continued with *At Land* (1945) and *A Study in Choreography for Camera* (1945) and closed with *Ritual in Transfigured Time* (1946). This last film came just before Deren's protracted engagement with Haiti and Vodou begun in 1947. Her original plan was to make an ethnographic film on Haitian rituals and dance, a project suggested by Margaret Mead and Gregory Bateson's innovative ethnographic work in Bali, which used the camera as a research tool. Deren's efforts, though lasting years and resulting in miles of footage, never came together in a completed film. All kinds of practical problems, plus Deren's overinvolvement as a "participant observer," which included her initiation as a Vodou priestess, contributed to the project's growing incoherence. There was Deren's book *Divine Horseman: The Living Gods of Haiti* (1953), edited by Joseph Campbell, and there were later attempts by other hands to assemble the dance and ritual footage. When she returned to New York, *Meditation on Violence* (1948) and *The Very Eye of the Night* (1958) never drew the admiration her first cycle of films had excited. The usual take was that Deren had an interrupted career, cut short by her early death at forty-four in 1961. This familiar account is what Keller sets out to challenge.

Keller seeks to show the incomplete Deren as, in some crucial ways, the real Deren. She recalls that film history is strewn with unfinished and abandoned works, taking Orson Welles as her chief example. Closer to Deren, however, are some more compelling examples—provided by Sergei Eisenstein, whose own ethnographic quagmire with the never-finished *¡Que Viva Mexico!* pulled him down from the pinnacle of international reputation to years immured in a Soviet classroom, or Deren's contemporary Kenneth Anger, maker of *Fireworks* in 1947 and likewise working in Los Angeles, whose career is pocked with fragments of unfinished works (like *Puce Moment,* the long-abandoned *Rabbit's Moon,* and the fragment of *Kustom Kar Kommandos*).

What does Keller achieve using incompletion as an operative concept? Basically, she reimagines Deren's life itself as an aesthetics project, with films finished and uncomplete likewise contributing to a life in art. In one fascinating chapter, she treats the film *Witch's Cradle* that Deren attempted right after *Meshes,* following her move from Los Angeles to New York, and puts her in the circle of the city's avant-garde, notably, Roberto Matta and Ann Matta-Clark, Marcel Duchamp, and Peggy Guggenheim's museum Art of This Century. Its gallery was to provide the set for *Witch's*

Cradle. Keller discusses the project at length, digging deep into the archive of outtakes, stills, and scripts, as if the film existed, more or less. The chapter is richly suggestive but does not change the fact that Deren never found a solution to how to shoot it. What remains, emblematically from Duchamp, are the chess pieces that appear as a furtive motif in her next film, *At Land.* So, typical of Keller's book, the reader learns a good deal about Deren's intellectual biography and her artistic and intellectual engagements in the years after *Meshes.* As an odd kind of interpretive biography, it proves to be at once very insightful and unpersuasive.

Barbara Hammer presents a different challenge. She made many films for many different purposes. Her intellectual life was mercurial at best, and her aesthetics varied significantly from year to year, though she never wavered from a full-on sincerity. Hammer seems to have been eager to release everything she made and apparently abandoned nothing. Keller's solution this time is a more conventional one than she used with Deren: she divides Hammer's career into three periods corresponding to decades of her career—the 1970s, as a tyro autobiographer-filmmaker who fast became a lesbian cinema pioneer; the 1980s, as an ambitious experimental artist seeking and gaining recognition from the art world; and the 1990s, as a lesbian cinema historian-memorialist. Keller's organization of the material is therefore fairly straightforward: the first films were intensely personal, as with *I Was/I Am* (1973), a film that Keller (supported by Hammer) compares to *Meshes.* But there is little sense beyond this film that Hammer would really follow Deren's example. For one thing, Hammer discovered rapid editing early and would soon find superimpositions, split screens, and painting on film to be important for her, and she later "fell in love" with the optical printer (she bought one in 1983). Deren eschewed all such surface interferences with the image, and whereas Hammer's films tend to be giddy with antic energy and sexy provocation, Deren's films remained solemn and rather austere. Early on, Keller writes, Hammer "investigates images of herself in a rich variety of forms" (24), and she was interested in screen equivalents to touch, the body, sexual transport, and sensuality. In short, Hammer's

films depart in fundamental ways from Deren's formalism and her commitments to a clear and unimpeded cinematography. Hammer's more proximate precursor (as noted by Jennifer Barker) should be the fiery multimedia artist and filmmaker Carolee Schneemann. And Hammer is contemporary with the wave of punky film artists like Abigail Child and Peggy Ahwesh, a connection Keller makes (through Erika Balsom) but does not pursue. Keller observes that when Hammer's filmmaking spread from self-portraiture into lesbian celebrations, centered on naked bodies, on freestyle movement, on sex and a social happiness, these garnered Hammer the "distinction of pioneering such representations in experimental film" (54). While some of these films of the 1970s have not weathered well, several, like *Double Strength* (1978), show Hammer's rising confidence and control with framing and pacing, as well as skill with the handheld camera.

Nevertheless, Hammer was unsatisfied with her early success. She was aware of the constrictions her San Francisco setting placed on her work, and, ever ambitious, she desired recognition beyond her role in lesbian activism. So she moved to New York in the 1980s, and though she confronted the formalist side of experimental filmmaking head-on, she arrived too late for a timely meeting with "structural film." That movement dissipated before Hammer got to New York. But it is clear Hammer was quick to develop a more technical and exacting style—or styles, really, because she pulled devices like flicker effects and optical printing from structural filmmakers and seldom rested in a single form for more than a film or two. Hammer's previous fans were, Keller reports, disappointed by this new experimentation, not just by the aggressive formality she pursued but, more to the point, by the notable drop-off in lesbian imagery and rhetoric tempest.

Hammer's career then rises from the delicate *Pools* (1981), a film that bears comparison to Marie Menken's *Arabesque for Kenneth Anger* (1969) in using decorative elements of a location—in this case, the neoclassical swimming pools that architect Julia Morgan designed for Hearst's Castle—up to *Optic Nerve* (1985), a film that mixes flicker effects with a studied portrait of Hammer's aged grandmother and is overlaid with a sophisticated sound assembly. With these films, Hammer was achieving aesthetic control and exhibiting an advanced taste in forward techniques, not in film after film, but hitting often enough to grant her substantive authority as an experimental filmmaker.

Keller's method rests on close descriptive scrutiny. She makes a fine companion to a reader who seeks to see Hammer whole and through a clear-eyed and elaborately informed critical lens. Though she is generally reluctant to interpret, usually letting the always voluble Hammer be the book's thematic guide, Keller zeroes in on her artistic project and shows it developing. If Hammer had her doubts about structural film even as her own films reworked its devices—her complaint is that those films lacked emotion—it is certainly not true of *Optic Nerve,* which uses highly controlled means to convey the pathos of Hammer's grandparent.

By the end of the 1980s, and now receiving recognition, grants, and invitations to high-profile screenings, Hammer restored a new activism to her filmmaking with *Snow Job: The Media Hysteria of AIDS* (1986), the mockery of *No No Nooky TV* (1987), and the provocation of *The History of the World According to a Lesbian* (1988). These are admirably abrasive bits of agitprop, but they are minor, haphazard works.

Then, in 1990, there was another turn in Hammer's career: she discovered the archive. When she was shown Dr. James Sibley Watson's X-ray films, Hammer was inspired. Watson and his colleagues developed these for medical work in the 1950s, but, on their own time, they made a set of X-ray films of ordinary actions, such as drinking milk and shaking hands. Keller is astute in assessing how strongly these films registered with Hammer, as if she had found something crucial she never knew she was looking for. Obviously astonished, Hammer brings her own fully developed strengths (including a new feature, tact) to this already fascinating material. Her rhythmic sense, her color and reframing, are all marshaled to make the wordless *Sanctus* (1990) a marvel. Keller devotes one of her longest and most probing discussions to it. *Sanctus* has two companions: Keller dismisses the documentary *Dr. Watson's X-Rays* (1990). The mostly black-and-white *Vital Signs* (1991), in which Hammer shows herself dancing with a skeleton intercut with blurry shots from *Hiroshima mon amour,* is also bad, though Keller indulges the film by interpreting it as a manifestation of Hammer's growing interest in the body's frailties and death. Still, Hammer would soon make much stronger films drawing on archive materials—the X-ray film is her first to do so—and she would also seek a documentary format that works.

Nitrate Kisses is the film where all this happens and initiates Hammer's third and last major phase (the 1990s). At sixty-seven minutes, it is regarded as Hammer's masterwork. The film also presages her cycle of historian-memorialist lesbian films that would punctuate the decade with its high points. *Nitrate Kisses* is set out in terms of four gay couples gradually having sex, each belonging to one of four generations spanning the century. The film begins with novelist Willa Cather and ends with two punk lovers festooned in chains and leather. These episodes are all intercut with scenes from Dr. Watson's other important archival contribution to Hammer, *Lot in Sodom* (1933). Codirected with Melville Webber, and one of the George Eastman Museum's archival treasures, this silent feature is a fantastic, gay avant-garde "biblical" epic. However, no one at the time seems to have noticed the gay aspect as such. In addition to the historically sequential portraits of lovers, Hammer's film is joining her own queer cinema to the first American avant-garde's queer masterpiece. Unlike most of Hammer's previous films, *Nitrate Kisses* also has notable textual accompaniment, including a long quotation intertitle from Michel Foucault's *History of Sexuality* and another from Walter Benjamin's "Theses on the Philosophy of History." Indeed, a significant portion at the center of the film concerns attempts to recover the real history of the repression and persecution of lesbians by the Nazis.

The cycle of documentaries that flow from *Nitrate Kisses* and follow its format quite closely includes *The Female Closet* (1998), portraits of three lesbian artists over a century, and *History Lessons* (2000), a film that uses old black-and-white film clips, sex cartoons, book covers, and wild TV announcers intercut with a young lesbian couple having enthusiastic sex; the film varies the thesis (that Vito Russo originated in his 1981 book *Celluloid Closet*) that you can find lesbians in many places if you know what to look for. As these later films appear and grow longer and more declamatory, they indicate Hammer's commitment of memory as her late form for her rediscovered lesbian activism. They may lack the spontaneously defiant erotic glee of *Dyketactics* with which Hammer kickstarted her work, but these films are the result of an artist who broke out of the parochial limits Hammer once felt to commend a wide circle of viewers. They sealed her reputation and made her an important presence at film festivals.

If we pass through *Maya Deren: Incomplete Control* without ever sharing Keller's conviction about her novel thesis, we proceed through the companionable *Barbara Hammer:* *Pushing Out of the Frame* feeling that Keller has taken the most generous measure of this filmmaker and the best of the many works this prolific filmmaker made. Having perhaps previously known Hammer only as a marginal art world personality, this book reveals a filmmaker seen in relief.

Bart Testa is an associate professor (teaching) in the Cinema Studies Institute, University of Toronto. Testa is the author of *Back and Forth: Early Cinema and the Avant-Garde* (1992) and coeditor of *Pier Paolo Pasolini: Contemporary Perspectives* (1994). He has contributed articles and reviews to a variety of journals and anthologies, including "An Axiomatic Cinema" in *Michael Snow: Presence and Absence* (1995).

   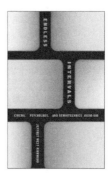

ONE-STOP SHOP
FILM INSPECTION & SCANNING

It has always been our standard policy to inspect film prior to scanning. As a full-service provider of film restoration and archiving services, PRO-TEK Vaults offers meticulous cleaning, inspection, repair, and high resolution motion picture film scanning with the Lasergraphics Director 10K — all under one roof.

With the combination of the most skilled film technicians, digital technology, and best practices, you gain the highest quality results and greatest satisfaction.

PRO-TEK
V A U L T S

protekvaults.com